Divine Revelation

A Secret Look into Heaven

GERALDINE M. COOL

Order this book online at www.trafford.com
or email orders@trafford.com

Most Trafford titles are also available at major online book retailers.

King James Bible, by Royal Publishing, copyright 1971, and the Everyday
Bible, New Century version, copyright 1987, 1988, 1991 by Word Publishing.

Printed in the United States of America.

ISBN: 978-1-4907-4400-1 (sc)
ISBN: 978-1-4907-4399-8 (e)

Library of Congress Control Number: 2014914315

Trafford rev. 09/04/2014

 www.trafford.com

North America & international
toll-free: 1 888 232 4444 (USA & Canada)
fax: 812 355 4082

DEDICATION

I DEDICATE THIS BOOK TO my Lord and Savior Jesus Christ who has given me beautiful insights of heaven. Without my Lord and Savior I would be nothing.

INTRODUCTION

I DECIDED TO WRITE THIS book to share some of my experiences that God allowed me to have. Before I accepted Christ as my Savior, there were several times that I attempted to take my own life. One time I almost succeeded. Through this entire God saw something worth saving and he patiently waited for me. Heaven is a reality and this I know for sure. There was no way I seen everything in heaven because that would have taken an eternity. Some day- when heaven is my home I will see and experience the things I did not on this short sojourn. In 2 Corinthians 12: 4, it tells us that there are things in heaven that no human is allowed to tell. In this same chapter, verse 9, we are told by God, 'My grace is sufficient for you…' After many prayers and tears this is the result. My prayer is that as the book becomes disturbed it will cause many souls to come to know Christ as their Lord and Savior, so they may make preparations to spend eternity in heaven. Join with me in spreading the wonderful message that Jesus is coming soon. The Lord has wonderful things in store for us here on earth and then in heaven.

Sharing this message is something I am grateful for to God. These experiences have strengthened and encouraged me. I pray God will bless you all.

This book is very important because we are living in the end time and every soul on earth needs to know how wonderful heaven is.

TO GERALDINE FROM JESUS (insert your name here)

You were born for a purpose and now it is time to fulfill that purpose. What I have shown and told you I want you to record, write and tell. All these things are true and faithful. Your important mission is to tell the world that there is a heaven and a hell. Tell them I was sent by the Father and that from torment, I came to save them, so that they may prepare a place in heaven.

INSIDE THE GATES

I LAY IN THE HOSPITAL dying from an overdose of medication. Slowly, I felt myself dissolving into oblivion. Suddenly I felt the power of Almighty God fall upon me. A mighty angel stood by my bed with the Lord stood behind him. I looked into the face of Jesus, but he said not a word

The angel spoke and said he was a messenger of God. He said to me 'God has given me a special mission and that mission is to take you to heaven and show you parts of it.

Standing there for a moment he then said 'Come and see the glory of God.

I left this earthy plane and found myself in a beautiful place called heaven. The detail of my sojourn to heaven from my hospital bed is unclear to me. But no way can I be mistaken of the reality of it. As I stepped onto the heavenly shores the Lord was there to meet me with outstretched hands. He embraced me lovingly and I could feel the love flowing from him to me, for it was very intense. After awhile, which seemed like a long time, he held me at arm's length and looked into my eyes with great love. He said to me 'My child, I will manifest myself to you so you may bring people out of their darkness into light. This is the purpose I have chosen for you. The things I tell and show you are too recorded and written.

Yielding myself completely to God amazing things began to happen. As he released me from his arms I was taken down to the pits of hell. This gesture greatly surprised me. Here in hell I was conscious of all five of my senses, hearing, tasting, smelling, feeling and seeing. I knew this was a supernatural happening. The impact it made on me was for a purpose

Being in hell grieved my heart because of the horrors I seen. These horrors saddened and burdened my heart. I was able to see the judgment of God on sin and on the people who had gone to hell. Praying earnestly I sought God's comfort.

I was lifted up and immediately transported to the entrance of heaven

Even here on the outside of heaven's gates the beauty was astonishing. In fact, the beauty was so amazing it took my breath away. My mighty angel was clothed with a sparkling garment of light. His triangle shaped wings were a kaleidoscope of colors. I was not surprised but very much amazed with the wonder of the indescribable beauty of God that was evident all around

My angel repeated an exclamation I would hear many times, "Come and see the glory of God!'

In front of me was a magnificent gate made of solid gold. In fear and reverence I took in everything I could of this awe-inspiring sight. Nowhere in sight was the Lord, but I was totally enraptured by heaven's glory.

ENTERING HEAVEN

*S*TANDING AT THE GATES of heaven were two mighty angels with glistening robes and their hair spun like gold. In their hands they held swords. The angel who was guiding me on my journey stepped away from me and went over to the two angels. That left me standing alone thinking how glorious the gates of heaven were. For me this was wonderful to see.

The realization came over me that the gates of heaven had opened.

Some of the conversation the angels were having I could hear. Leaving my angel and the other one standing at the gate, one of the angels stepped inside of the gate and came back with a book. I could see that the cover was gold. The angel held up the book for me to see and I seen these words written across the cover.

"Geraldine's Life History."

The angel who had carried the book now opened it, studied it for a moment, and with a smile of approval said to me 'You may now enter through the magnificent gates of heaven.' my guiding angel and I walked through the gate

Upon entering I could hear music that filled the whole atmosphere and penetrated my whole body. Enveloping everyone and everything wave after wave of beautiful music and singing rose and fell across the landscape

Astonishment at what I seen inside the gates was awe-inspiring and was beyond description. I stood there gazing at the most beautiful flowers that I had ever seen, they were so colorful. Even the blooms seemed to be alive to the heavenly music. The music swirled around me and I became a part of it. No description could describe the beauty of the city---the joy I will share with you is quite another thing.

Coming towards me were citizens of the great city, among them were my grandfather, parents, a niece and my younger sister and they were all clothed in white robes.

Isaiah 61: 10: "I will greatly rejoice in the Lord, my soul shall be joyful my God; for He has covered me with the robe of righteousness, as the bridegroom decks himself with ornaments and as a bride adorns herself with jewels."

Beyond comparison was the happiness and joy that shined brightly from their faces.

Heaven is a prepared place for prepared people. As children of God we have been transformed and through the miracle of regeneration have been made anew. Now that we are new creations in Christ, joy fills our souls knowing that the place we will spend eternity will be with our Savior Jesus Christ who saved us.

Heaven is a real place. It is not a figment of someone's imagination. Jesus said and it is recorded in John 14: 1-3: "Let not your heart be troubled: ye believe in God, believe also in me. In my Father's house are many mansions; if it were not so, I would have told you. I go to prepare a place for you."

Heaven is a perfect place. It has to be perfect because our Savior is perfect, almighty and eternal. Since God is preparing a place in eternity for us to live with him, our eternal home will be perfect.

Isaiah 57: 15: "…I dwell in the high and holy place…"

Nobody or nothing will spoil the beauty of our heavenly home and never will there be anything allowed entering heaven to defile or damage it.

Revelation 12: 3-4, 7-10 and 12-13 tells us about Michael and his angels being cast out. "And another sign appeared in heaven: behold a great, fiery red dragon having seven heads and ten horns and seven diadems (crowns) on their heads. His tail drew a third of the stars (angelic hosts) of heaven and threw them to earth. And the dragon stood before the woman who was to give birth, to devour her child as soon as it was born.

And war broke out in heaven: Michael and his angels fought with the dragon and the dragon and his angels fought, but they did not prevail, nor was there a place found for them in heaven any longer.

So the great dragon was cast out, that serpent of old, called the Devil and Satan, who deceives the whole world; he was cast to the earth and his angels were cast out with him.

Then I heard a loud voice saying in heaven "Now salvation and strength and the kingdom of our God and the power of his Christ have come, for the accuser of our brethren, who accused them before our God day and night, has been cast down.

Therefore, rejoice O heavens and you who dwell in them. Woe to the inhabitants of the earth and sea. For the devil has come down to you, having great wrath, because he knows that he has a short time. Now when the dragon saw that he had been cast to earth, he persecuted the woman who gave birth to the male child."

In the sacred (holy) and pure climate of heaven, the serpent, Satan, and his unholy associates (cohorts) will never again rear their ugly heads because the demons are evil and they cannot enter heaven

Jude 1: 6: tells us "And the angels who did not keep their proper domain, but left their own abode, he has reserved in everlasting under darkness for the judgment of the great day." This verse talks about the fallen angels who rebelled against God.

Here on earth there are obvious faults and flaws in our homes keeping us from being perfect.

In heaven we will lack nothing because no detail will be left out to keep heaven's environment from being perfect.

The place called heaven is constructed by God, so there are no mistakes. There is no human comprehension that can describe the beauty and wonders of heaven. It is beyond our human power to describe. OH!! That beautiful place, the indescribable splendor is marvelous to behold.

The untold number of mansions reflects walls of jasper and gates of pearl are combined with the brilliance of the light of the Son of God. 1 John 1: 5: "…God is light…" Revelation 22: 5: "…neither light of the sun; for the Lord God giveth light…"

No artist could portray or create a scene that could adequately describe the beautiful River of Life. In Revelation 22: 1-3: we read "And he shewed me a pure river of water of life, clear as crystal, proceeding out of the throne of God and of the Lamb. In the midst of the street of it, and on either side of the river, was there the tree of life, which bare twelve manners of fruits and yielded her fruit every month: and the leaves of the tree were for healing of the nations. And there shall be no more curses: but the throne of God and of the Lamb shall be in it…"

HOME OF THE REDEEMED SOULS

*H*EAVEN IS OUR PERMANENT home and no enemy will ever conquer God's paradise. The buildings will never crumble or decay. The vegetation will never wither and die. Heaven is an abiding, eternal and continuing city.

All Glory to God—I am a Child of the King. That is the glorious realization of all.

In that matchless place, saints will find pleasant deliverance from all our disappointments, disasters, tragedies, heartaches, sorrow and woe. In heaven there will be no crying or pain.

Revelation 21:4: says "And God will wipe away every tear from their eyes; thee will be no more death, nor sorrow nor crying. There will be no more pain for the former things have passed away." And in verse 5 it says "I will make all things new…"

In heaven there are numerous nationalities—red, yellow, black and white to name just a few. Everyone was joyful. Seeing this diversity of people Revelation

5: 9 came to mind. It says "You are worthy to take the scroll and to open its seals; for you were slain and have redeemed us to God by your blood out of every tribe and tongue and nation."

EMPLOYED IN PRAISING GOD

I WAS SO EXCITED IN the majesty of God that my soul praised him. Heaven was being revealed to me. What I had been revealed about hell, the sorrows I experienced, the grief and suffering now seemed far away. The revelation concerning hell brought this scripture to mind. Mark 9: 48: "In hell the worm does not die, the fire is never put out." In Revelation 14: 11 it tells us "And the smoke from their burning pain will rise forever and ever

Together we are entire families. Every face I saw glowed with happiness. The saints in heaven seemed to be occupied, going somewhere, doing something and always smiling. Not one person was idle. Their time was spent magnifying, praising and singing songs to their Lord. The dominant mood of music filled the air

Do not think that once you reach heaven that your time will be spent in leisure, you're badly mistaken. No sitting idly, no floating on clouds or lazily sitting on the banks of the River of Life wiggling your toes in the water. Our time, in heaven, will be occupied in service to God. We cannot say what nature of this service will be. But one thing is for sure—that Gods people will serve him.

DIAMONDS FOR SOUL WINNERS

*A*S FAR AS THE eyes could see there were exquisite, sparkling diamonds. Some of the diamonds were as large as cement blocks. These large diamonds were used for the mansions of the ones who had been soul-winners on earth. Heaven provided a diamond for the faithful Christian every time that person led someone to Christ.

Proverbs 11: 30 says "The fruit of the righteous is a tree of life and he who wins souls is wise

Daniel 12: 3: "Those who are wise shall shine like the brightness of the firmament and those who turn many to righteous as the stars forever and ever."

As I stood absorbing the great brightness and majesty of the splendid place, I saw an immense, beautiful angel coming towards me. My heart gave a flutter because of his immense size. In his hand was a scroll with gold edging around it.

There was a pedestal table made of silver material, unlike anything I had ever seen, which sparkled with light. Upon this table the angel placed the scroll. I got a glimpse of the scroll and seen a name written on it. One of the many saints was allowed to pick up the scroll and then was instructed to begin reading it. 1 Corinthians 3: 11 "The foundation that has already been laid is Jesus Christ and no one can lay down any other foundation." The saint turned towards me and said "Jesus is the Master builder and he decides who deserves the diamonds and where they go. In this scroll is a report of someone who led others to Christ, who fed the hungry, clothed the poor and naked and who did wonderful things for God."

Matthew 25: 31-41 and 46 says "The Son of Man will come again in his great glory, with all his angels. He will be King and sit on his great throne. All the nations of the world will be gathered before him and he will separate them into two groups as a shepherd separates the sheep from the goats. The Son of Man will put the sheep on his right and the goats on his left.

Then the King will say to the people on his right, come, my father has given you his blessing. Receive the kingdom God has prepared for you since the world was made.

Matthew 25: 35-36: "For I was an hungered and ye gave me meat, I was thirsty and ye gave me drink: I was a stranger and ye took me in: Naked and ye clothed me: I was in prison and ye came unto me." The Everyday Bible phrases it like this "I was hungry and you gave me food. I was thirsty and you gave me something to drink. I was alone and away from home and you invited me into your house. I was without clothes and you gave me something to wear. I was sick and you cared for me. I was in prison and you visited me. "Then the good people will answer 'Lord, when did we see you hungry and give you food, or thirsty and give you something to drink? When did we see you alone and away from home and invite you into our house? When we see you without clothes and give you something to wear? When did we see you sick or in prison and care for you?'

Then the King will answer, 'I tell you the truth, anything you did for even the least of my people here, you also did for me.'

Then the King will say to those on the left 'Go away from me, you will be punished. Go into the fire that burns forever that was prepared for the devil and his angels. These people go off to be punished but the good people will live forever.' Matthew 25: 46.

ROOM FOR EVERYONE

'COME AND SEE THE glory of God.' the angel repeated.

All of us need to understand the focus of our wishes and desires is to spend eternity in heaven with the Lord. Heaven is the land of dreams.

Excitement fills my heart because I know, for surety, that when my works on earth are finished, I will leave this earth and enter heaven. Isaiah 57: 15: "…I will dwell in the high and holy place…" God has prepared the city for the ones who love him and do his work.

At this time I would like to insert a special little note here. The angel had a surprise for me. She said to me 'Look who is coming down the street to greet you.' it was my precious sister, Alice, who had died from cancer. Running up to me she embraced me tightly in her arms and said 'My dear sister, it is so good to see you again.' That said she disappeared in the twinkling of an eye.

PERFECT COMMUNION

ETWEEN GOD AND MAN unbroken fellowship will be completely restored in heaven

While Adam and Eve lived in the Garden of Eden, God visited them frequently. The fellowship was broken with Good because Adam and Eve disobeyed and sinned. But God desires continually to have communication with mankind.

God's ultimate expression of love for mankind was giving his only son to die a merciless death on the cross. The possibility of fellowship between God and man became possible through Christ's death.

The circumstances in our lives can hinder our intimate relationship with God. There will be no hindrances in heaven. Fellowship with God will be complete and we will know complete fellowship with the King of Kings and Lord of Lords.

Heaven is the dwelling place of our living God. Heaven is far above atmospheric heavens, beyond the planets and the Milky Way. It is the immortal home of 'the redeemed of the Lord.' Isaiah 62:12: "His people will be called the Holy People, the Saved People of the Lord."

Our mansions in heaven will not be a tiny cubicle, so we have nothing to fear about being crowded. Our mansions will be glorious. When the saved of the Lord are assembled in the home of glory, there will be enough room for everyone to have a mansion, no crowding.

John 12: 1-4: "Let not your heart be troubled; you believe in God, believe also in me. In my Father's house are many mansions; if it were not so, I would have told you. I go to prepare a place for you. And if I go and prepare a place for you, I will come again and receive you unto myself; that where I am, there you may be also. And where I go you know and the way you know."

There is definitely room enough for everyone in heaven.

Revelation 7: 9-11: "After the vision of these things I looked and there were a great number of people, so many that no one could count them. They were from every nation, tribe, people and language of the earth. They were all standing before the throne and before the Lamb, wearing white robes and holding palm branches in their hands. They were shouting in a loud voice "Salvation belongs to our God, who sits on the throne and to the Lamb." All the angels were standing around the throne and the elders and the four living creatures. They were all bowed down on their faces before the throne and worshiped God."

TEARS IN HEAVEN

*A*s THE ANGEL WAS guiding me through heaven we stopped at a particular place. She said to me 'God wanted me to show you this room of tears.'

Psalms 56: 8: "...Put my tears into your bottle. Are they not in your book?"

The angels catch each tear; we shed, and bottle them. There are many who have shed tears for their loved ones, children, spouse and family. Many tears have been shed because of separation or divorce and you felt all hope was lost and you grieved over your loved ones. The room of tears was so beautiful. I was taken to the entrance which had no door. Peering through the opening I could see it wasn't very large but this room radiated with power and holiness and the sight was overwhelming. Inside this room were shelves lined with crystal and glowing with light. As I looked at the shelves there were many bottles that were clear glass. In front of each bottle there was a plague with a name written on it. I was not allowed in this room because of the power and holiness that was within it.

Out of the corner of my eye, I saw a man who seemed to be glorified. His deep-colored robe looked like velvet and was very beautiful. In the middle of the room there was an elegant table which was made of valuable material and glowed with a brilliant light. I was greatly surprised at the very abundant display. On this table there were books sewn with beautiful silk-like material and were intricately made. Some of the books had pearls, diamonds and lace on them, while others had purple and green stones on them. These books intrigued me and my attention was drawn to them. I was entranced as I stood there.

OH! Lord, these books are so beautiful. I love books so these books attracted my attention. I was overwhelmed and wonderment overcame me as I looked steadily around.

My attention was drawn to the scene that I did not realize someone had come up behind me. A gentleman tapped me on the shoulder and said 'Come with me. I want to show you more of this room and explain to you about the tears. There are many rooms like this but this specific room, I am in charge of.' An angel came through the entrance as the man was talking to me. His wings were large and a kaleidoscope of colors and his stature was a least twelve feet tall. The angel's majesty and beauty left me in awe. His robe was brilliantly white with gold trim all the way down the front. This vast angel held a golden bowl in his hands which contained a liquid.

Revelation 5:8: "...golden bowls of incense which are prayers of Gods holy people." The man said to me

'From earth the angel has brought me a bowl of tears. Now I want you to see what we do with them.'

The angel handed the man the bowl and a piece of paper. Written on the piece of paper was the name of the person who had shed the tears. The man went over to the shelves where the bottles were kept and matched the name on the paper with the name on the plague. These were the tears of that person. Taking the bottle off the shelf, the man brought it over to the bowl and poured the tears into the bottle.

Before continuing the man said to me 'Tell the people on earth about this. I want to show you what we do with the tears.'

After filling the bottle with tears, he picked up one of the books and told me to look. Looking upon the book the pages were blank. The keeper of the room said to me 'These are the tears that God's saints cry. See what happens.' Watching as he poured a tiny teardrop from the bottle, immediately words began to appear on the whole page and the writing was beautifully and elegantly written. Page after page this process, of dropping a teardrop on the page was continued and every time the teardrop hit the page words would appear.

Without mentioning what was written on the pages, the keeper closed the book. He then said to me 'The most perfect prayers are those that are bathed in tears that come from the souls of men and women on earth. Tell the people on earth about this.

Then the angel with the beautiful rainbow colored wings said to me "Come and see the glory of God."

GOD OPENED THE BOOK

EFORE I KNEW WHAT was happening we were transported to a very large place with thousands of people and heavenly beings. In heaven a person is moved around from one place to another effortlessly. This place is beyond beautiful, so much so it can't be explained. As I stood there in awe the people seemed to fade away and God's glory appeared everywhere. Thunderous were the praises to God. I was escorted to the throne of God by a heavenly messenger.

There was a huge cloud and within this cloud I saw an image of a being. I could not see God's face, but the glory of God was visible and there was a rainbow over the throne. Out of the cloud came the voice of God as described in Revelation 14: 2: "I heard a voice from heaven like the voice of many waters, and like the voice of loud thunder."

Around the throne there were many horses with riders. In front of God's throne a book mystically appeared on the altar and angels who were gathered around the throne bowed down before God. Fear and reverence filled the scene. As I stood there a hand came out of the cloud and opened up the book. Deep within my heart I knew it was the hand of God who had opened the book.

Ascending from the book, I was greatly surprised to see what I thought was smoke. Surrounding the area where I stood the most beautiful smell engulfed the area. My guiding angel, who had been by my side the whole time, said to me--" This book contains the prayers of the saints." She went on to say that God was sending his angels to answer the prayers from the cries of the hearts. All around me every man, woman, child and heavenly beings were praising and magnifying God.

Once God opened the book, pages began to fly into the hands of the angels on horseback. Like the voice of thunder I heard God command the angels 'Go answer her prayer, go answer his prayer and go answer the prayers of the children.

Psalms 56: 8-11: "Thou tellest my wanderings: put thou my tears into thy bottle: are they not in thy book? When I cry unto thee, then shall mine enemies turn back: this I know, for God is for me. In God will I praise his word? In God have I put my trust: I will not be afraid what a man can do unto me."

In the living word of God, he explains what he does with our tears. How marvelous it is to understand the glory and wonder of our God and how marvelous it is to be on the receiving end of God's compassion. He really cares for the tears we shed.

There are numerous scriptures that speak about tears, sorrows and God's comfort for us.

2 Kings 20: 5: "Thus says the Lord, the God of David thy father, I have heard your prayers, I have seen your tears, surely I will heal you."

Isaiah 66: 13: "As one whom his mother comforteth, so will I comfort you…"

2 Corinthians 1:3: "Blessed be the God and Father of our Lord Jesus Christ, the Father of mercies and God of all comfort."

Psalms 116: 8: "For you delivered my soul from death, my eyes from tears and my feet from falling."

Isaiah 25: 8: "He will swallow up death forever and the Lord God will wipe away tears from their faces."

Psalms 126: 5-6: "Those who sow in tears shall reap in joy. He, who continually goes weeping, bearing seed for sowing, shall doubtless come again with rejoicing, bringing in the sheaves."

Psalms 86: 17: "Because you, Lord, have helped and comforted me."

Jeremiah 31: 16: "Refrain your voice from weeping and your eyes from tears; for your work shall be rewarded, says the Lord and they shall come back from the land of the enemy."

Isaiah 35: 10: "And the ransomed of the Lord shall return and come to Zion with singing, with everlasting joy on their heads… They shall obtain joy and gladness and sorrow and sighing shall flee away."

Revelation 7: 17: "The Lamb who is in the midst of the throne will shepherd them and lead them to living fountains of waters and God will wipe away every tear from their eyes: for there shall be no more deaths, nor sorrow, nor crying. There shall be no more pain, for the former things have passed away."

I pray these scriptures have uplifted you.

Glory to God in the highest for heaven is a real place and we as servants of God will be going there. When we go to heaven we will not be vapors of smoke floating on clouds.

Once we are in heaven our tears and sorrows will be replaced with eternal joy. God has promised us this in his word and much more.

THRONE OF GOD

I CANNOT EMPHASIZE IT ENOUGH!!!!!! ***Heaven is real.*** It is a literal destination. It is not some short lived dream or imagined vision. Through the Holy Scriptures God reveals to us many of the actual existence of heaven.

THE FIRST HEAVEN (Physical Heaven)

The first heaven is the atmosphere around the earth called the atmospheric heaven. This area is where birds fly and the winds blow. The first heaven is where showers, thunderstorms, fog, vapor and clouds are formed.

Rev 14: 7: "Saying with a loud voice, Fear God, and give glory to him; for the hour of his judgment is come: and worship him that made heaven and earth and the sea and the fountains of waters."

In Acts 1: 11, the angel was referring to the sky when he ask the disciples why they were gazing up into heaven.

Hebrews 1: 10: "And Thou, Lord, in the beginning hast laid the foundation of the earth: and the heavens are the works of thine hands."

Isaiah 45: 12: "I have made the earth and created man upon it; I even my hands, have stretched them out and all their host have I commanded."

John 17: 1: says Jesus lifted up his eyes to heaven (toward the sky).

SECOND HEAVEN

This is a heaven of space. This space is the region of the sun, moon and stars. The Bible mentions the second heaven in many places. Here are but a few of them.

Isaiah 13: 10: "For the stars of heaven and their constellations will not give their light; the sun will be darkened in its going forth and the moon will not cause its light to shine."

Matthew 24: 29: "Immediately after the tribulation of those days the sun will b darkened and the moon will not give its light; the stars will fall from the heaven and the powers of heaven will be shaken."

Genesis 22: 17: "Blessing, I will bless you and multiplying I will multiply your descendants as the stars of the heaven and as the sand which is on the seashore."

Deuteronomy 4: 19: "And take heed lest you lift your eyes to heaven and when you see the sun, the moon and the stars, all the host of heaven, you feel driven to worship them and serve them, which the

Lord your God has given to all the peoples under the whole heaven as a heritage."

Job 38: 31-33: "Can you bind the cluster of the Pleiades or loose the bands of Orion? Can you bring out Mazzaroth in its season? Or can you bring the Great Bear with its cubs? Do you know the ordinances of the heavens? Can you set their dominion over the earth?"

THIRD HEAVEN

The third heaven is the destination of the righteous and it is far beyond the region of the sun, moon and stars

In 2 Corinthians 12: 2, the apostle Paul, refers to this place when he wrote "I knew a man in Christ above fourteen years ago (whether in body, I cannot tell; or whether out of body, I cannot tell; God knoweth); such an one caught up in the third heaven.

Heaven is the region often spoken of as the immediate presence of God.

Hebrews 9: 24: "For Christ has not entered the holy places made with hands, which are copies of the true, but into heaven itself, now to appear in the presence of God for us."

God lives in heaven.

In Matthew 6: 9, Jesus taught us to pray---praying "Our Father which art in heaven…"

Psalms 11: 4 is called Gods holy temple and the place where the throne is…" The Lord is in his holy temple; the Lord sits on the throne in heaven…"

Isaiah 6: 1: "I saw the Lord sitting on a very high throne…"

Lamentations 3: 41: "Let us lift up our hearts with hands unto God in heaven…"

And in 1 Kings 8: 30 heaven is called the dwelling place of God--" "And hear thou in heaven thy dwelling place…"

The dwelling place of the righteous is called a garner; Matthew 3: 12.

The Kingdom of Christ and of God, Ephesians 5: 5.

The Father's House, John 14: 2. A Heavenly Country, Hebrews 11: 16.

A Rest, Hebrews 4: 9 and Revelation 14: 13.

Paradise, 2 Corinthians 12: 2 and 4.

In the temple is God's divine majesty.

Hebrews 1: 3: "Who being the brightness of his glory, and the express image of his person and upholding all things by the word of his power, when he had purged our sins, sat down on the right hand of the Majesty on high."

In the most remarkable manner God's excellent glory is revealed. It is a holy place of light, joy and glory. The exact location of heaven is not known but we often refer to it as 'being up there'

Beyond a shadow of a doubt we know that God Almighty is in heaven. There in heaven God and Jesus Christ are the central point of saints, angels and all worshiping beings. In heaven we will be in glorious company with the angels. In Matthew 18: 10, Jesus said "In heaven angels always see the face of my Father who is in heaven."

Jesus promised us saints in John 14: 3 that "Where I am, there you may be also…"

1 Peter 1: 4 tells us an inheritance has been reserved for us in heaven; an inheritance that is incorruptible undefiled and will not fade away.

It is very exciting to share with you all the beauty of heaven. During my visit to heaven I saw many things and so many people.

THE PRAISE OF HEAVEN

MY CONSTANT ANGEL, WHO had been with me from the start and had shown me the room, said to me "Come and see the glory of God."

The shining, magnificent splendor of heaven overwhelmed me. The blazes of glory seemed to shoot from everything I saw, filled me with awe. Without seeing this no one could picture, in their minds the beauty and blessedness of heaven.

Once said by an anonymous person—

The light of heaven
        is the face of Jesus.
The joy of heaven
        is the presence of God.

Everywhere I could feel happiness, joy and peace as I journeyed with my angel. She seemed to know my thoughts. My angel said to me "You have a mission to fulfill for God and that is to tell people what is up here. God has shown you some of heaven, but not all of it.' She repeated the exclamation of 'Come and see the glory of God.'

Suddenly my ears heard singing of many voices singing praises to God. My soul was thrilled with the magnificent music of worshipers. Glory and honor echoed and re-echoed through the wide expanse of heaven as seraphim (high order of angels) and the saints sang endless songs of praise with great abundance.

APPROACHING THE THRONE

A s I NEARED THE throne of God my soul was made lively and carried away with joy. The angel, who had guided me through my journey in heaven, stopped and told me we were not going any farther. In front of me I could see a continuous scene of events taking place. The same scene that John saw in a vision, I saw. Revelation 5: 11-13 tells us about this vision. "And I beheld and I heard the voice of many angels round about the throne and the beasts and elders; and the number of them was ten thousand of ten thousands; Saying with a loud voice, Worthy is the Lamb that was slain to receive power and riches and wisdom and strength and honor and glory and blessing. And every creature which is in heaven and on the earth and under the earth and such as are in the sea and all that are in them, heard I saying, Blessing and honor and glory and power, be unto him that sitteth upon the throne and unto the Lamb forever and ever."

There is no way people on earth can realize what God has in store for us who love him.

As I looked long and steadily, in great joy, something more remarkable happened. The voices of the thousands and thousands became louder and louder, almost deafening.

I was surprised that the angel had permitted me to see the throne of God, for this had been a dream of mine for a long time.

THE GLORIOUS THRONE OF GOD

*I*SAIAH 6: 1: "I saw the Lord sitting upon the throne, high and lifted up and his train filled the temple." Flowing in its beauty and purity the River of Life came under its base.

Revelation 22: 1-3: "And he shewed me a pure river of water of life, clear as crystal, proceeding out of the throne of God and of the Lamb. In the midst of it and on either side of the river, was there the tree of life… but the throne of God and of the Lamb shall be in it." The glory of God overpowered the throne.

Psalms 19: 1: "The heavens declare the glory of God…" Lightning, thunder and voices were all around the throne.

Revelation 4: 5 describes a vision John had of heaven. "And out of the throne proceeded lightning and thunder and voices and there were seven lamps of fire burning before the throne, which are the seven Spirits of God."

Overwhelming the throne was the most beautiful rainbow, I had ever seen.

Revelation 4: 3: "And he who sat there was like jasper and a sardius stone in appearance and there was a rainbow around the throne, in appearance like an emerald.

The magnificent, sparkling hues of the rainbow were mixed with light, bringing forth dazzlingly intense colors. This rainbow was far beyond anything I had seen on earth. Different hues of color radiated light signifying glory and power and a bright display of great brightness flashed from the throne.

Revelation 21: 23: "...for the glory of God did lighten it, and the Lamb is the light thereof."

Radiating from the rainbow were beams of glory—much of heaven seemed transparent and the illuminating beams that came forth from the throne were filled with light and reflected every part of paradise.

I stayed in this heavenly room for a long time, how long I really do not know. I was so overwhelmed with the wonder that time did not matter. Standing in this awe-inspiring place I thought of the thousands and thousands who were already in heaven because of their faith.

Luke 13: 24: "Strive to enter in at the strait gate..."

The holiness of God, the purity of his grandeur (majesty) and the projection of his word, I was thinking about.

I shouted at the top of my lungs, "OH! Lord, my God, how wonderful it is to see your glory, majesty and power."

I became aware that my guiding angel was at my side. She said to me "Come with me. God wants me to show you many other things in heaven."

THE ROOM OF RECORDS

*I*N THIS ROOM THE records were contained. They were extremely, excessively and carefully cared for. Each and every detail was kept.

The angel ask me "Do you know that God keeps records of every church service on earth and every service held in homes of saints that are praising and uplifting the Lord?"

It came as a surprise that God kept records of those out of his will, also.

I was shown how God kept track of the money that was given in the church services and the attitudes in which each person gave. There are other people who have money but will not give to the work of the Lord.

Mark 12: 41-44 tells us about a widow and her offering. "Now Jesus sat opposite the treasury and saw the people put money into the treasury. And many who were rich put in much. Then one poor widow came and threw in two mites (one-fifth of a cent) makes a quadran (two mites' equals' one quadran or farthing. Jesus called his disciples to himself and said to them, "Assuredly, I say to you that this poor widow has put in more than all those who have given to the treasury, for they all put in out of their abundance, but she out of her poverty, put in all she had, her whole livihood."

Luke 21: 1-4 reiterates the story of the widow.

Numerous things were revealed to me on my journey to heaven, including the 'records room. This guiding angel reminded me that I was to remember the things I had seen and experienced and to make a record of it. She also told me I was seeing some things dimly because they are mysteries to me.

1 Corinthians 13: 12: "For now we see in a mirror, dimly, but then face to face. Now I know in part, but then I shall know just as I also am known."

Ephesians 1; 9; 'Having made known unto us the mystery of his will, according to his good pleasure which he hath proposed in himself..."

The angel again reiterated the fact that I was to share what I had seen and experienced there in heaven with the people on earth. Quickly I was taken to another part of heaven which had a very long corridor. These corridors and walls were very high and they appeared to be made of platinum. Ringing out continually were the high praises of God. From the wall such brilliance reflected that I was filled with awe and reverence. The walls appeared to be a mile long for I could not see the end of it.

THE STOREHOUSE OF GOD

"*L*OOK AT THE TOP of the wall," the angel instructed me. I looked up and there on top I seen this word written. ***"Storehouse."*** "What are these rooms," I ask the angel.

The angel informed me that these rooms were the rooms where blessings are stored up for God's people.

Ephesians 1: 3: "Bless be the God and father our Lord Jesus Christ, who has blessed us with every spiritual blessing in the heavenly places of Christ…"

James 1: 17: "Every good gift and every perfect gift is from above…"

The angel also told me that these rooms contain blessings that are stored up for God's people.

1 Corinthians 2: 9: "…eye has not seen nor ear heard nor have entered into the heart of man the things God has prepared for those who love him"

HEAVEN IS A PERFECT PURITY

S O THAT WE MAY enjoy heavens atmosphere God wants to purify his saints on earth.

1Timothy 5: 22 says "…keep yourself pure."

Psalms 51: 10: "Create in me a clean heart, O God…"

Heaven is full of joy.

Psalms 16: 11: "…in your presence is fullness of joy…"

It is God's desire to give us, his saints, fullness of joy.

Heaven is eternal freedom. While we are on earth, God desires greatly for us to have deliverance.

Galatians 5: 1: "Stand fast therefore in the liberty by which Christ has made us free."

1 John 3: 3: "And everyone who has his hopes in Him purifies himself, just as He is pure."

1 John 3: 5-6: "And you know that He was manifested to take away our sins and in Him there is no sin, whoever abides in Him does not sin…"

Heaven is completely complete. While we are living on earth God wants us to feel confident and secure. It is God's desire to heal his saints on earth.

Here are but a few of the scriptures that show God wants to heal us.

1 Peter 2: 24: "...by whose stripes ye were healed."

Luke 5: 17: "...and the power of the Lord was present to heal them."

Exodus 15: 26: "...I am the Lord that healeth thee."

James 5: 16: "...the Lord will raise him up..."

Acts 9: 34: "Jesus Christ heals you..."

Isaiah 53: 5: "...and by His stripes we are healed

Heaven is a realization of hopes and satisfaction and it is Gods desire for us to be satisfied on earth. In the Lord's Prayer in Matthew 6: 10-13 we are instructed to pray that 'Gods will be done on earth as it is in heaven.' God wants us to have a sampling of heaven on earth. For us, God's saints, there are storehouses of blessings for us. These blessings are waiting for us to claim and receive here on earth. God wants to save you.

1 Timothy 1: 15: "...Jesus Christ came into the world to save sinners..."

Hebrews 7: 25: "Therefore He is also able to save to the uttermost those who come to God through Him..."

He wants to heal you.

He wants to deliver you.

He wants you to know 'the peace of God which surpasses all understanding. Philippians 4: 7: "And the peace of God, which passeth all understanding, shall keep your hearts and minds through Christ Jesus."

God wants you to experience a lasting joy. 1 Peter 1: 8: "rejoice with joy unspeakable."

THE HEALING JESUS

*T*HE ANGEL LOOKED ME in the eye and said "Come and see the glory of God."

Suddenly the angel disappeared and Jesus appeared by my side.

As I looked at him, his stature seemed larger than I had imagined. His eyes sparkled like diamonds, his scarred feet were graced with sandals, his sparkling white robe hung elegantly and was beautiful in form, his face glowed like the morning sun and his hair shone with radiance.

"What are these rooms?" I ask as I stood gazing into his eyes. Without speaking a word, the Lord stretched forth his toward the wall. As he did so, a large opening appeared. From this large opening flowed forth glory, power and light, seemingly giving glory to God.

'OH! Lord, what is this?" I cried.

His answer to me was 'These are for my people, my child. This glory, power and light is for sinners on earth if they will only believe. I died on the cross to make them whole. Romans 5: 8: "But God commandeth his love toward us, in that, while we were yet sinners, Christ died for us."

Looking into his loving eyes I knew he wanted everyone to believe that he, Jesus Christ, died so we could be made whole.

James 5: 15: "And the prayer of faith will save the sick and the Lord will raise him up…"

Isaiah 38: 16: "…so you will restore me and make me live…"

Psalms 103: 3: "…who heals all your diseases?"

God told me 'For the people on earth miraculous healings are waiting. Such an avalanche of miraculous healings will occur in days to come.'

Continuing the talk with me, God said, 'Child, there are storehouses and supply buildings as far as the eye can see, waiting for those who believe and receive. Believe I am the Lord Jesus Christ and that I am able to do these things and all they have to do is reach out and receive my gifts.'

1 Corinthians 14: 1: "…desire spiritual gifts…"

James 1: 17: "Every good gift and perfect gift is from above and cometh down from the Father of lights…'

Looking me squarely in the eyes God stressed to me that when I returned to earth I was to remember that healing is not from you, my child, nor is the vessel that heals. Just speak my word, pray and I will do the healing.

James 5: 16: "Confess your faults one to another and pray one for another, that ye may be healed. The effectual fervent prayer of a righteous man availeth much."

Believe!!! Believe that the Lord Jesus can and will heal you. *Glory to God!!!*

Hallelujah!!!

Thank You, Jesus!!!

Lowering his hand, the opening in the wall closed. After God closed the opening the angel swiftly took me to another place. This place was filled with music and wondrous praises to God. One of the songs, I heard, that they were singing can be found in Revelation 15: 3-4: "… great and marvelous are your works, Lord God Almighty. Just and true are your ways, O King of saints! Who shall not fear you, O Lord and glorify your name? For you alone are holy. For all nations shall come and worship before you. For your judgments have been manifested."

BEFORE, NOW AND AFTER

I HAD OFTEN WONDERED ABOUT many things and now I was getting answers

The angel begin to reveal many things to me and related many great mysteries

1 Corinthians 15: 51: "Behold, I tell you a mystery…"

Ephesians 1: 9: "Having made known to us the mystery of his will…"

The angel said to me 'the Lord spoke to me and said I was to show you before, now and after. You will be greatly excited at the things I am going to show you. I am going to reveal to you what happens when a person is born again. Also I will show you how a persons sins are washed away in the records room.

Revelation 1: 5: "…to him who loved us and washed us from our sins in his own blood."

Hebrews 10: 17: "…their sins and lawless deeds I will remember no more."

Titus 3: 5: "…according to his mercy he saved us through the washing of regeneration and renewing of the Holy Ghost."

Acts 22: 16: "Arise and be baptized and wash away your sins, calling on the name of the Lord."

When a born again individual dies on earth and that persons soul enters heaven, I have the great joy in showing you what happens.

The angel then said to me "Come and see the glory of God." Immediately we were off at a very fast pace, faster than the speed of light and in an instant we were back on earth. As in a vision I could see the earth.

"Look and behold," the angel told me.

Allowing the vision to pass before me the angel allowed me to see a small, beautiful, rural church. This church looked like it was in the country, but where it was located, I do not know. Through the vision I could see the inside of the church and seated in the pews were Gods holy people. I could hear the people shouting 'Amens' and 'Hallelujahs' as the pastor preached on Isaiah 55: 6-7. "Seek the Lord while he may be found. Call upon him while he is near. Let the wicked forsake his ways and the unrighteous man his thoughts; and let him return unto the Lord and he will have mercy upon him and to our God, for he will abundantly pardon."

Gazing upon this scene, I saw a mighty angel surrounding the church. A look of bewilderment passed over my face. Sensing my bewilderment this angel ask me, 'Do you know that a large angel is stationed at every church and that each of these angels are in charge of all the other angels of the church?'

Acts 7: 38: "This is he that was in the church in the wilderness…"

ANGELS AT CHURCH

*O*N THE OUTSIDE OF the church door stood two mighty angels. There were people coming and going and were not aware of the angels. As my guiding angel waved her hand, the roof seemed to magically open.

Around the pastor and the pulpit stood four angels. One on each side of the pastor and two just beyond them were the other two. A couple scriptures passed through my mind.

Psalms 84: 4: "Blessed are they that dwell in thy house, they will be still praising thee."

Hebrews 10: 25: "Not forsaking the assembling of ourselves together…"

Standing behind the congregation, in the back of the church, were two more angels. About halfway up the aisle stood two more angels and up near the altar stood two more angels. I was greatly surprised at the number of angels that were in the church. Several of the angels had pens and scrolls in their hands.

'Why do some of the angels have pen and scroll?' I ask the angel.

'Come I will show you what happens.' the angel replied.

The pastor prayed a prayer over the collection plate and then it was passed around. The angels with pens and scrolls recorded each person who gave and their attitude as they gave. On each scroll the angel recorded each contributor's thoughts. Also written was if they gave begrudgingly or if they gave because they loved the Lord and wanted to give to the work of the Lord or enjoyed giving the offering and viewing it as a act of worship. All these thoughts and actions were written on the scrolls.

2 Corinthians 9: 7: "Each one should give as you have decided in your heart to give. You should not be sad when you give and you should not give because you feel forced to God. God loves the person who gives happily."

Acts 20: 35: "…it is more blessed to give than receive."

Matthew 6: 4: "…your giving should be done in secret; your Father can see what is done in secret, and he will reward you."

For a reason unknown to me, the angels nodded their heads at each other.

All the activity that was happening was invisible to the people of the church, but I could everything clearly.

Tapping me gently on my shoulder my guiding angel said 'I want to show you something else. You will be greatly blessed—so watch closely.' In the blink of an eye I found myself behind the pastor. I recognized the scripture he was preaching on. Isaiah

55: 6: "Seek ye the Lord while he may be found, call upon him while he is near."

Mingling inside the church was a number of angels and during the entire service these angels were rejoicing. Looking at the preacher as he delivered the message I could tell he was under the anointing of the Holy Spirit. One of the angels nearest the pastor was pouring something that looked like fire upon his head. Every word the preacher spoke was for the glory of God.

Suddenly my attention was drawn to the front door of the church, which opened noisily as a very drunk man came staggering in and without stopping or looking around he headed for the altar. It was as if an invisible force was propelling him forward. Stopping in front of the altar, he interrupted the preacher and said 'Preacher, I am an alcoholic and for so long alcohol has controlled my life. Because of my addiction I have lost everything, family, friends, work. The drunk fell to his knees and started pouring his heart out to God. He cried out in a loud voice 'Be merciful to me a sinner.' Luke 18: 13: "God be merciful to me a sinner

As he knelt there a couple deacons went up to him and put their arms across his shoulder. One of the deacons ask the man 'Are you serious about wanting to be saved? And do you mean business with God?'

The man screamed 'Yes, oh, yes, I want to be saved. I have been an alcoholic for as long as I can remember. I desperately need to be saved.'

With the assurance that the man meant what he was saying, the deacons led the man onto victory.

A SOUL IS SAVED

*I*MMEDIATELY TWO ANGELS APPEARED near the man. Both of the angels had scrolls in their hands and began writing what this alcoholic man had said. The deacons that were knelt next to the man led him through the process of salvation. This man's life had been filled with sins of every conceivable kind. Now by his confession of faith his sins were forgiven.

Isaiah 1: 18: "…though your sins be as scarlet, they shall be white as snow; though they be red like crimson, they shall be as wool."

An amazing thing happened as the deacons were praying with the man. An angel touched the man's heart and smoke as black as the pits of hell came spewing out his chest.

As I stood there some scriptures came to my minds that talk about the vile sins that come out of the heart.

Matthew 15: 18-19: "But what people say with their mouths comes from the way they think; these are the things that make people unclean. Out of the mind come evil thoughts, murder, adultery, sexual sins, stealing, lying and speaking of others."

Matthew 12: 35: "Good people have good things in their hearts and so they say good things. But evil people have evil in their hearts, so they say evil things."

Jeremiah 17: 9: "The heart is deceitful above all things and desperately wicked: who can know?"

Raising his hands unto the Lord I could see black bands wrapped all around him. This man was in bondage to all types (kinds) of sins, especially his drunkenness and alcoholism. 'You must confess your sins to God, so that he can forgive you and so you can be washed in the blood of the Lamb,' one of the deacons told him.

1 John 1: 9: "If we confess our sins, he is faithful and just to forgive us our sins."

Romans 10: 9: "If you use your mouth to say 'Jesus is Lord' and if you believe in your heart that God hath raised him from the dead, you will be saved."

The man began to confess his sins one after another. I watched as an angel touched him and as he did I saw fire coming from the hand of the angel. Band after band of sins that had enwrapped him burst off. I could see a tremendous liberty fill the man.

Galatians 5: 1: "Stand fast therefore in the liberty wherewith Christ has made us free."

Colossians 1:14: "The Son paid for our sins and in him we have forgiveness…"

Raising his hands, this man praised the Lord. Coming down upon the man was the glory of God. As this once drunken man stood up I knew that the Lord had sobered him up, because he began to shout and sing the praises of God.

The two angels that had been with him and recording his words nodded with satisfaction. These two angels walked back to where my guardian angel and I stood, turned to me and said; "Come and see the glory of God."

IN THE RECORDS ROOM AGAIN

VERY SWIFTLY THE TWO other angels, my guardian angel and I traveled back to heaven. A beautiful pathway of gold appeared before us after we entered through the gates. Once on the pathway we were transported to a beautiful room.

"Come and see what we do here." I was told.

I noticed along the pathway there were others rooms similar to the one we were entering.

My guardian said to me; "In heaven there are many rooms and these rooms are called 'Rooms of Records.' What goes on in rooms, you are being given the opportunity to see what goes on in these rooms."

'The room I am going to show you is of the man we seen converted on earth. His name is written in that room. Entering the room where the man's name on was, I saw the angels that had been on earth with us, moving very fast towards another angel. The report the angels had written on earth was now handed over to this angel.

Positioned along the walls, in this spacious room, there were ladders extending to the ceiling. On every wall there were shelves and upon these shelves were books.

This is like a library on earth, I thought to myself.

Standing in front of a large desk were many angels singing and praising God. The desk was large, long and narrow. My estimation of this desk would be eight feet long by four feet wide. The desk was overlaid in gold and in the center of the desk there was a cutout with fruit and leaves. I could not take my eyes off this table because it was so beautiful. I could never imagine anything as beautiful as this desk. Nothing on earth could compare to the beauty of this desk. Angels went up and down the ladders retrieving books from the shelves and placing them in their right place. Close at hand were other angels with reports they had collected from around the world. I observed different shades of and wondered why, but did not ask. Standing in line were the two angels I had seen at the country church and in the hand of one of them was a book. I learned this was the book of the man who I had witnessed being born again.

'Do you remember these two angels?' I was asked by my guardian angel.

'Yes, I remember them.'

'Do you know what is in the book they hold in their hands?'

'No.'

'The book they hold in their hands is a record of the man who was saved in the country church. It was retrieved from the shelf so it can be taken to the angel in charge.'

In every record room, there is an angel in charge, my guide explained. That angel sees everything that goes in or out of that particular room. To glorify the glory of God, everything is done in order.

Sudden wonder overtook at everything I seen.

The angel in charge of this room wore a tiara that sparkled with a heavenly brilliance. His pure white robe glistened with gold and his colored wings were at least twelve feet across. This beautiful angel was the record keeper of this particular room.

My guardian angel motioned for me to come to him and by some unseen power, I found myself at his side.

'I am to tell you something,' he said to me. You have been given these insights so you can see what happens when a person is born again. God has permitted you these insights so you could share with the people on earth the joys and benefits of being born again.' The wonder of this experience sent a shivering, exciting feeling through me.

KEEPING RECORDS

*A*LL AROUND ME WERE high praises to God. Psalms 66:2: "…make his praises glorious."

Psalms 7: 17: "…and sing praise to the name of the Lord most high."

For his glorious acts and wondrous power, I began to praise and magnify God.

It startled me when I felt a tap on my shoulder. It was my angel and he had a question.

'Do you see the angels in front of the desk?'

'Yes, I do.'

'These angels were present when the man in the country church was born again.'

These three scriptures came to mind.

Proverbs 20:22: "…wait on the Lord and he shall save thee."

Ephesians 2:8: "…you have been saved by the grace through believing."

1Timothy 1: 15: "…Christ Jesus came into the world to save sinners

Out of the scroll he pulled a message but I could not see what was written on it. My curiosity must have shown on my face because my angel asked if I would like to see what was written on the scroll.

Oh, yes was my reply.

As he handed me the scroll he told me to look at what is written in it.

Looking at the message on the scroll, I seen it was very beautiful and written in an orderly manner. Written in this scroll was the name of the country, the state, the county, the city and even the name of the church. Also written in the scroll was the name of the pastor and the amount of people in the church. The order in which the service was conducted was also recorded in this scroll. Everything that went on in the service was recorded. As I read farther down, the scroll, I read about the people who had taken part in the service and there were details on the offering.

As I read through the scroll I saw the name of the man who had been saved in the country church. The exact time to the very second of this man's conversion was written, in detail, on the scroll. This man was saved because of a pastor who was not afraid to preach the gospel of the Lord Jesus Christ.

I could not help but shout, 'Glory to God, Glory to God.'

I knew that every one of us will have a record, either good or bad that will be written in scrolls.

As this written account got to the point where the man prayed the sinners prayer and accepted Jesus Christ as Lord and Savior, the angel in charge ask the two other angels, 'At the time and hour that this man was born again, did you witness it?'

In unison they answered yes that they were there and witnessed the once drunken man as he was saved and received Jesus Christ as his Lord and Savior. We saw his conversion happen.'

Amazingly, shouts, praises and noises of glory went up. Everyone in heaven was magnifying God.

Luke 18: 13: "...God be merciful to me a sinner."

Luke 15: 10: "...there is joy of the angels of God over one sinner that repenteth."

Romans 5: 8: "...while we were yet sinners Christ died for us."

The angel wrote something in the book and then closed it. This book about the man was very thick.

'Look behind you;' my guiding angel instructed.

There behind me were a multitude of redeemed saints all dressed in white, robes adorned in brilliance.

THE BLOOD OF JESUS

T HE SONG THE REDEEMED were singing was one I often sang in church.

'Nothing but the blood of Jesus can wash away my sins. Nothing but the blood of Jesus can make me whole today. Nothing but the blood of Jesus can cleanse me today. I've been redeemed by the blood of the Lamb.'

In the Word of God there are scriptures that tell us to sing praises.

Psalms 95: 1: "O,'come; let us sing unto the Lord."

Ephesians 5: 19: "…singing and making melody in your heart to the Lord."

Psalms 100: 2: "…come before his presence with singing."

Hebrews 2: 12: "…I will sing praises unto thee."

Revelation 14:3: "…they sung as it were a new song before the throne."

As I watched one of the rejoicing angels was handed the man's book. It looked, to me, to be a very thick book, but as I watched in awe, each and every page of the old writings was washed away. By the blood of Jesus each and every page was cleansed and made pure as it was lifted up. Now nothing of this man's sins remained. As I witnessed this cleansing I thought of a couple scriptures.

Isaiah 43: 25: "I, even I, am he who blots out your transgressions, for my own sake and remembers your sins no more.'

Isaiah 44: 22: "I have blotted out…thy sins…for I have redeemed thee."

Lord, your magnificent word marches on. By the precious blood of Jesus this man's sins were washed away.

An exchange of the book took place, as I stood watching. This large book was placed upon a tray that was being held by an angel who had the most beautiful, shining long hair. The brilliance of the morning sun could not compare to this angel's hair. Shouts of praises and glory went up as this book was placed upon the tray. My guiding angel said;' Come and see the glory of God.'

No sooner had he spoken these words I found myself traveling, at a rapid pace through the corridors of heaven.

THE LAMB'S BOOK OF LIFE

OMING TO A STOP, I found myself before the throne of God. Trumpets blared and horns blew. Around the entire area, around the throne, a cloud of glory, the Shekinah glory illuminated. (Ezekiel 9: 3). (SHE-KINAH: The visible sign of God's presence on the ark of the testimony in the land of holies).

Exodus 25: 22: "And there I will meet with thee and I will commune with thee from above the mercy seat, from between the two cherubims which are upon the ark of the testimony…"

Leviticus 16: 2: "…I will appear in the cloud upon the mercy seat…"

A multitude of voices sang, Glory to God!!! Hallelujah!!!

Enraptured with this powerful scene I watched as an angel laid the book on the altar of the Lord and then bowed low.

I heard the resonating voice of God, through the air, as he shouted; 'Another soul has been redeemed by my son's blood. Through the blood of my son another person has received eternal salvation.'

Isaiah 45: 17: "...shall be saved in the Lord with an everlasting salvation..."

Bowing low before the Lord I began praising God as the bells of heaven rang. Every person in heaven shouted.

On the altar of God, I saw the Lamb's Book of Life.
Revelation 20: 12: "...the book of life..."

From out of a cloud came a hand and opened the book, which had been lain on the altar. In the Lamb's Book of Life, the once drunken man's name was written.

Glory to God!!

If we are saved and baptized in the blood of Jesus we become saints and our names are written in the Lamb's Book of Life.

Revelation 21: 27: "...written in the Lamb's Book of Life..." 'Come and see the glory of God,' the angel said. At the speed of light I was taken out of heaven. As I flew with the angel this passage came to mind.

Isaiah 45:3-4: "I will give you the treasures of darkness and hidden riches of secret places that you may know that I, the Lord, who call you by your name am the God of Israel. For Jacob my servant's sake and Israel my elect, I have even called thee by thy name. I have surnamed thee, though thou hast not known me."

RIVER OF LIFE

*T*HE NEXT SCENE WAS of the Lord taking the saints of the living God through the River of Life. The River of Life flows from the throne of God and the Lamb.

Revelation 22: 1: "And he shewed me a pure river of water of life, clear as crystal proceeding out of the throne of God and the Lamb."

All the saints shouted; *Glory to God*.

An innumerable company of saints were being clothed in the purest, whitest and most magnificent robes ever seen by man.

In Revelation 7: 13-14, John wrote "Then one of the elders answered, saying to me, 'Who are these arrayed in white robes? And where did they come from? And I said to him, "Sir, you know." So he said to me, "These are the ones who come out of the great tribulation and washed their robes and made them white in the blood of the Lamb."

BEFORE THE THRONE

EFORE ME AT THE throne of God, I witnessed an exciting, awesome scene. Standing where few have stood, at the throne of God, I heard trumpets blaring. There are no words, in the English language that could describe adequately the fear, reverence and thrill I felt.

Twelve angels adorned in garments, far beyond any earthly description stood in front of the throne. On the breastplates of their apparel, and in their garments jewels were imbedded. Adorned upon their heads was a heavenly material with a rainbow of colors. The long robes were adorned with gold edging.

One by one the saints were announced by the blare of the trumpet to stand before God. Making up the huge gallery were an inestimable number of angels, heavenly beings and saints. All were glorifying God shouting 'Glory to God, Glory to God.'

REDEEMED ONES

*T*HE REDEEMED OF ALL ages were glorious and beautiful. The redeemed were real people, not clouds floating in space nor were they puffs of smoke.

The angels continuously praised God's majesty in unbroken voices.

As I was standing before the throne of God I heard a mighty voice saying, "Behold, the tabernacle of God is with men and he will dwell with them and they shall be his people. God himself will be with them and be their God." Revelation 21: 3.

From a cloud of glory came lightning, thunder and voices. Suddenly I saw the hand of God coming out of the cloud wiping the tears from the eyes of the saints.

Isaiah 25: 8: "...the Lord God will wipe away tears off all faces..."

Revelation 21: 4: "God will wipe away every tear from their eyes."

I heard the voice of God saying; "There shall be no more death, nor sorrow, nor crying. There shall be no more pain, for the former things have passed away." Revelation 21: 4-5.

To all the saints that were gathered together God said; 'I see your names are written in the Lambs Book of Life. Welcome into the joy of the Lord. "Well done, good and faithful servant, you were faithful over a few things, I will make you ruler over many things. Enter into the joy of the Lord." Matthew 25: 21.

God placed a magnificent golden crown upon the heads of each and every sanctified person.

For all the redeemed the blessings of God will continue and never end.

STOREHOUSES OF HEAVEN

I REALLY BELIEVE THIS VISIT to heaven was to give me a balance. God knew of my many visits to hell and how horrifying it was for me. Through his love he gave me this blessing of seeing heaven.

I was shown God's storehouses during my visit to heaven. Blessings upon blessings were stored here until a saint prayed and ask God for a blessing. Through the love and mercy of God blessings would be bestowed upon that saint.

An angel said to me; 'Come and see the glory of God.'

This angel was tall and beautiful. His rainbow colored wings was shaped like triangles. This particular angel was instructed, by God, to show me different parts of heaven.

Higher and higher through the atmosphere we traveled until we came to the entrance of heaven again. The first thing that caught my eyes was the fruit trees loaded with beautiful fruit and the families dressed in beautiful attire. Up and down a hillside families were shouting praises to their Lord and King.

Saturating the environment was the most beautiful and melodious music you would ever want to hear. Heavenly music is a manifestation of pleasure and gladness (joy). This manifestation is an evidence of happiness.

On earth I had heard some beautiful choirs but nothing on earth can compare with the beauty and splendor of the singing and music in heaven.

Heaven is a full orchestra of music. If you can, for a moment imagine millions of perfectly pitched voices singing sweetly the melodies of heaven. Not one person was off key. Everything and everyone was in perfect harmony.

All types of stringed instruments, along with trumpets and other types of musical instruments provided beautiful music. The voices of the redeemed, who were praising God with great joy, blended harmoniously with the combination of musical instruments. By the power of the Almighty God, the musical sound of the instruments, like the singing voices were purified and made perfect.

I was enraptured hearing the extraordinary praises to God. In heaven, the ones of us that cannot carry a tune, in singing, will sing in beautiful harmony. There will be such happiness in heaven. There is nothing on earth that can compare to the grand and eloquent music of the celestial city.

Wave after wave of majestic anthems of praise filled the air throughout every street in heaven and through the landscape. It surrounded me so completely that I could not hear or think of anything for quite sometime.

Finally my guiding angel tapped me on the shoulder and said; 'Come and see the glory of God.'

The area I found myself in had the greenest grass that I had ever seen.

In certain parts of the grass there were clusters of the most beautiful flowers. These flowers were gorgeous and reminded me of roses. Every one of the flowers had a bloom consisting of magnificent petals.

Luke 12: 27: "Solomon in all his glory was not arrayed like one of these."

To me it looked like the flowers were singing.

HORSES IN HEAVEN

*A*S WE TRAVELED ALONG on our journey we came to a pasture with the most magnificent and beautiful white horses. In the book of Revelation I remember reading about horses and how one day my Lord and Jesus would one day come astride a white horse. He will be leading the armies of heaven, who will also be riding white horses.

Revelation 19: 11-14: "Now I saw heaven opened and behold a white horse and he that sat upon him was called Faithful and True, and in righteousness he doth judge and make war. His eyes were as the flames of fire and on his head were many crowns; and he had a name written that no man knew, but he himself. And he was clothed with a vesture dipped in blood: and his name is called the Word of God. And the armies which were in heaven followed him upon white horses, clothed in fine linen, white and clean" These horses were magnificent looking, pure white, very royal and to me resembled huge statues that had been chiseled out of boulders. They were not chiseled but very much alive and real and their hooves were enormous. This was quite a sight to behold.

Talking to the horses was a woman dressed in the most beautiful robe. It glittered like diamonds and shone brighter than the morning sun. She directed the horses to bow their knees in praise to God. Simultaneously all the horses bowed their right knee in praise to God.

'Oh, how wonderfully beautiful,' I thought.

In the Bible there are scriptures telling us every creature in heaven and earth will worship God. Here are four of those verses.

Revelation 5: 13: "Every creature which is in heaven and on earth and under the earth and such as are in the sea and all that are in them, heard I saying, Blessing and honor, and glory and power, be unto him that sitteth upon the throne, and unto the Lamb forever and ever."

The Everyday Bible phrases it this way; "Then I heard all creatures in heaven and on the earth and under the earth and in the sea saying; To the one who sits on the throne and to the Lamb be praise and honor and glory and power forever and ever."

Philippians 2: 9-11: "Therefore God also has highly exalted Him and given Him the name which is above every name, that at the name of Jesus every knee should bow, of those in heaven and of those on earth, and of those under the earth, and that every tongue should confess that Jesus Christ is Lord, to the glory of God the Father."

Romans 14: 11: "For it is written, 'As I live, says the Lord, every knee shall bow to me and confess to God.'"

Isaiah 45: 23: "I have sworn by myself the word has gone out of my mouth in righteousness and shall not return, that to me every knee shall bow, every tongue shall take an oath."

The Everyday Bible phrases it like this: "I will make a promise by my own power and my promise is true; what I say will not be changed. I promise that everyone will bow before me and will promise to follow me."

Everywhere there was happiness, joy and peace as people praised God.

$\mathcal{I}$ NOTICED THAT MY ANGEL was no longer with me but that Jesus stood before me. He was much taller than me and he wore such a beautiful robe, that it stood out from the others. Jesus had beautiful piercing eyes and there is no word in the English language that can describe the tenderness in those eyes. His beard was neatly trimmed and his golden-brown hair was very thick and long. The beauty of the Blessed Savior was awe-inspiring and marvelous.   I was so overwhelmed by the sight of Jesus I wanted to praise, worship and bow down before him, my Lord of Lords, my King of Kings and my Lord Jesus Christ. All around Jesus glory and power bellowed.

STOREHOUSES OF HEALING

*O*N JESUS EYES WAS a troubled look.
    'What is it, my Lord?'
    'Look, child.'
He pointed towards a building which had a very large opening and this building reminded me of a storehouse. Glory and power with billows and billows of power flowed steadily from the opening.

'My Lord, What is this?'

'Do you see the healings in this storehouse? There are many more like this one.'

'Yes, Lord, I see the healings flowing from the opening.'

'All these healings are ready for saved children of God;' the Lord told me.

Our sufferings in life are tragic due to the world being bombarded with all types of sickness, diseases, physical afflictions, deformities and similar illnesses people suffer.

Everywhere you look, it is there. Walking up and down the corridors of any hospital or medical center you will see suffering. Visit the for aids, tuberculosis, cancer and other contagious wards, mental health hospitals, intensive care facilities, emergency rooms and numerous other places that take care of people in terrible, excruciating pain and you will see physical and mental anguish beyond endurance.

1 Corinthians 10: 13: "The only temptation that has come to you is that which everyone has. But you can trust God, who will not permit you to be tempted more than you can stand, but when you are tempted he will also give you a way to escape so that you will be able to stand it."

Psalms 41: 3: "The Lord will give him strength when he is sick and he will make him well again."

Because Adam and Eve did not listen to God and ate of the forbidden fruit, sickness is the result of their fall.

Genesis 3: 6: "…so she took some of the fruit and ate it. She also gave some of the fruit to her husband and he ate it."

Sickness is one of sins consequences. Many see sickness as a nuisance, a tragedy of our human condition or just a part of normal existence. BUT!!!! In reality it is a curse of Satan.

HEALING IN HEAVEN

OVERWHELMING IS OUR NEED for healing. Sickness is a corruption of God's will. In the economy of God sickness is an unnatural element. **SICKNESS** did not originate from God, nor does it come from heaven. Sin is from an evil source, not a good source.

James 3: 16: "For where envying and strife is, there is confusion and every evil work."

All diseases, sickness and suffering will be gone forever when we get to heaven. But we have ultimate redemption.

Romans 8: 18: "The sufferings we have now are nothing compared to the great glory that will be shown to us. Everything God made is waiting with excitement for God to show his children's glory completely."

Not even the worst suffering possible here on earth, is not worthy in comparison with the exceedingly wonderful glory that will be ours in the future (life after death).

Deuteronomy 18: 13: "Thou shalt be perfect with the Lord thy God."

In heaven we will have perfect bodies resting in Christ with no pain, no suffering nor any other physical afflictions. Just because we will have perfect bodies, once we get to heaven, does not mean we cannot have healing now.

One of the many names of God in the Bible is Jehovah-Rapha, 'the Lord our healer.' God made a special covenant of healing with his people. In Exodus 15:26god promised Israel; "If you diligently heed the voice of the Lord your God and do what is right in His sight, give ear to His commandments and keep all His statues. I will put none of the diseases on you which I brought on the Egyptians. For I am the Lord who heals you."

Sickness is part of the curse of sin but through his death on the cross, Jesus lifted the curse for believers through his atonement for sin.

Galatians 3: 13: "Christ took away the curse the law put on us. He changed places with us and put himself under the curse."

Suffering the wounds and bruises, Christ paid the price for sin. Christ became our Savior. Not only did his suffering pay for our sins, but it set up permanently (proved) and established the truth that Jesus is our healer.

Isaiah 53: 5: "But he was wounded for our transgressions, he was bruised for our iniquities, the chastisement of our peace was upon him and with his stripes we are healed."

HEALING IS FOR TODAY

*A*FTER JESUS WAS TAKEN up from the disciples, into heaven, the healing ministry of Christ did not cease.

The book of Acts is a continuation of everything Jesus began to do and teach.

Acts 1: 1: "…of all that Jesus began both to do and teach."

While Jesus was on earth he modeled a healing ministry and taught that healing is a part of the benefits of the kingdom.

Before Jesus returned to His Father, he instructed believers to go and heal the sick.

Here are some scriptures on healing.

Matthew 4: 23: "…healing all manner of sickness and all manner of diseases among the people."

Luke 9: 11: "…healed them that had need of healing."

James 5: 15: "And the prayer of faith shall save the sick and the Lord shall raise him up…"

Mark 16: 17-18: "And these signs will follow those who believe. In my name they will cast out demons;

they will speak with new tongues; will take up serpents; and if drink anything deadly, it will by no means hurt them; they will lay hands on the sick and they will recover."

Also read these other scriptures: Acts 4: 22, 3 John 2, Luke 9:6, Psalms 103: 3 and Matthew 10: 1.

In John 14: 14-15 Jesus told us; "If ye shall ask anything in my name I will do it. If ye love me, keep my commandments."

1 John 3: 22: "...and whatsoever we ask we receive..."

1 John 5: 14: "And this is the confidence that we have in him, that if we ask anything according to his will, he hears us."

Also read Luke 11: 9, Matthew 21:22, and Matthew 7: 7.

After Jesus had left I walked through the storehouses with my angel. There were untold numbers of storehouses.

I heard Jesus speaking to my spirit, even though he had left. These were the words he spoke to me; "My precious child, when you pray for somebody on earth, pray for them in my name. *REMEMBER* that you don't do the healing, *I DO*. Ask of me any kind of healing, heart trouble, broken bones, cancer and so much more and I will straighten crooked limbs and I will heal sick bodies.

Whatever you want me to do, ask in my name and I will do it. In these storehouses answers are waiting."

Jesus said he could not emphasis enough that the blessings in the storehouses were for his people. Soon, very soon Jesus said there would be an avalanche of healings in the world.

My thoughts went to all the healings on earth.

'Lord, how marvelous it is that you repair our bodies.'

As we all know as we age our bodies begin to deteriorate. We will never be entirely free from this consequence because it is a natural effect of sin. Even though we age God does not want us to spend our later years bedridden and incapable. His will for us is to be active and productive. Jesus died, on the cross, so we could be made whole.

Jesus Christ, the son of God shed his blood so we could be saved from hell. Our blessings, privileges and hope for health and wellness are in Jesus. The only hope for our well-being is Jesus Christ.

Hebrews 6: 19: "We have this hope as an anchor for the soul, sure and strong..."

SAINTS!!! I cannot stress enough that there are storehouses of unclaimed blessings in heaven, ready and waiting to be claimed by God's people who ask in faith and in the name of Jesus.

When Jesus was on earth he told us in John 14: 2: "I go to prepare a place for you..."

Heaven is the place God is preparing for us. John 14: 2: "In my father's house are many mansions..."

1 Corinthians 2: 9: "...eye hath not seen, nor ear heard, neither have entered into the heart of man, the things which God hath prepared for them that love him."

The Everyday Bible reads like this: "...no one has ever imagined what God has prepared for those who love him."

Heaven is so beautiful and it is full of beautiful things and they are more beautiful than anything on earth.

The thought of heaven thrills my soul when I am speaking or thinking about it. I thank God for the beautiful Word that he has given us, His children.

ORDER IN HEAVEN

THERE IS NEVER AN idle moment in heaven, for it is a busy place and is always filled with excitement and activities. The angels are constantly busying themselves doing something. Each activity they do is useful, industrious enterprises.

I want to tell you how I saw the angels as they worked in heaven. The angels were joyful, happy, energetic, never tired or never sad and were always praising Jesus.

The angels were not the only ones busy in heaven; the redeemed souls are busy as well. Exactly what the kind of work the redeemed souls did, I do not know. But you can be sure that in heaven no one will be idle. No one on earth has ever experienced the kind of work the saints are busy with. The tasks they are engaged in are exhilarating, satisfying and stimulating. These saints were constantly praising, worshipping, and doing the things God appointed for them to do.

Looking around I saw angels flying back from earth with reports. From all over the world they came with reports from church services, prayer meetings and ones who were worshipping in their homes.

In their hands the angels held white pieces of paper that looked like scrolls. Around the edges of each of the pieces of paper there was gold trimming. The angels would travel from one part of heaven to other parts sharing their reports.

1Corinthians 14: 25: "The secret things in their hearts will be made known. So they will bow down and worship God saying, 'Truly God is with you.'

HEAVEN'S POPULATION

*O*SAW SAINTLY MEN WEARING beautiful, illustrious white robes.

Isaiah 61: 10: "I will greatly rejoice in the Lord, my soul shall be joyful in my God; for he has clothed me with the garments of salvation, he has covered me with the robe of righteousness, as a bridegroom decketh himself with ornaments and as a bride adorneth herself with jewels."

In heaven I saw so many people with distinctive features that came from every nation on earth.

Zechariah 2: 11: "And many nations shall be joined to the Lord on that day..."

Revelation 7: 9: "After these things I looked and behold, a great multitude which no one could number, of all nations, tribes, peoples and tongues, standing before the throne and before the Lamb, clothed with white robes, with palm branches in their hands."

I was impressed greatly that everything in heaven was in an orderly manner and in their proper place. No matter the task it was done thoroughly, properly and with the highest degree of excellence. No activity was ordinary, no product was poor and no work claimed superiority.

Upon the holy hills of heaven, entire families were worshipping God ad without reserve their joy and happiness was uninhibited. These families eagerly desired to go and do marvelous deeds in the Lord's presence. This was such a beautiful sight.

No matter what was done, it was done, and it was all done in an orderly fashion.

Heaven is totally and completely free of impurities and imperfections. Everything was perfect. Unknown in the paradise of God are the alterations and changes we are familiar with here on earth. Filling the souls and bodies of all who were there was perfect joy and peace.

2 Corinthians 5: 2: "For this we groan, earnestly desiring to be clothed upon with our house which is in heaven."

PERFECT ORDER

*E*VERYTHING THAT HAPPENS IN heaven characterizes perfect, divine order and purpose. Engaging in continuous, joyful, excellent service were the saints and the angels. In heaven no one is ever bored or idle. Serving God day and night forever are God's children, angels and other heavenly creatures.

In our heavenly home we will have new bodies that never become weak, tired or filled with sickness.

2 Corinthians 3: 18: "...are changed into the same image from glory to glory even as by the Spirit of the Lord."

Fatigue will never be known in heaven. Our supernatural, glorified bodies will never lose their strength. Time is suspended and circumstances do not damage our minds, our wills or our bodies.

We must have a heavenly nature to engage in the business and pleasures of heaven.

2 Peters 1: 4 tells us this is what happens when we are born again. "Whereby are given unto us exceeding

great and precious promises: that by these ye might be partakers of the divine nature…'

In the Everyday Bible it says: "Through these he gave us the very great and precious promises. With these gifts you can share in being like God and the world will not ruin you with evil desires."

The eternal God designed and built the architecture of heaven. One block in heaven had very large buildings with extremely large impressive crowns of many jewels across the top. I did not enter any of these buildings, so I had no idea how many people lived in them. These buildings were majestic and spacious.

The Bible tells us that when we are laboring on earth for Jesus we are laying up treasures in heaven. Here are a few verses verifying this.

Luke 18: 22: "…thou shalt have treasures in heaven…"

Luke 6: 23: "…your reward is great in heaven…"

Revelation 22: 12: "And behold, I come quickly and my reward is with me, to give every man according to his work shall be."

Revelation 11: 16-18: "Then the twenty-four elders, who sit on their thrones before God, bowed down on their faces and worshipped God. They said 'We give thanks to you, Lord God Almighty, who is and who was because you have begun to rule! The people of the world were angry, but your anger has come. The time has come to judge the dead and to reward your servants, the prophets and your holy people, all who respect you, great and small. The time has come to destroy those who destroy the world."

CHARIOTS OF GOD

THE LORD, HIMSELF, BADE me to come and see more of the glory of God. I walked beside the Lord while we moved from one part of heaven to another.

The Lord instructed an angel to show me the chariots of God. The wheels on the chariot were so huge that it was beyond my comprehension on how to describe them. The rim and spokes were studded with emeralds, precious rubies and diamonds. Each side of the chariot had two wheels and the fronts of the chariots were low and open like a sleigh. Every chariot seemed like it was ablaze with fire, but was never consumed.

Isaiah 66: 15: "For behold, the Lord will come with fire and with his chariots like a whirlwind, to render his anger with fury, and his rebuke with flames of fire."

BODIES OF QUALITY

*O*N HEAVEN, THE FEATURES of all the people were beautiful and glorified. There was not a blemish on any of the people and they glowed with radiance.

I've heard it said that when we get to heaven we will be vapors of smoke. Well, saints that is far from the truth. We will not be vapors of smoke but will have a bodily form and features.

1 Corinthians 15: 51: "…we shall all be changed. In a moment, in the twinkling of an eye…"

1 Corinthians 15: 44: "It is sown a natural body; it is raised a spiritual body. There is a natural body and there is a spiritual body."

Revelation 4: 4 tells us there are elders around the throne. "Around the throne were twenty-four thrones and on the thrones I saw twenty-four elders sitting, clothed in white robes and they had crowns of gold on their heads."

The beautiful saints of God who had died and gone on before us are patriarchs of heaven. Eternal life is given to the saints by God and I was given the privilege of seeing them as they received their new, glorified bodies after the Resurrection.

In heaven, saints, we will be gloriously happy. While I was in heaven memories of home were far away from my mind. There will be no sorrow, sadness, nor grief.

Revelation 21: 4: "...there will be no more death, neither sorrow, nor crying, neither shall there be any more pain..."

I was delighted in the joy and was awed by his beauty.

Heaven will have no darkness.

1 John 1: 5: "...God is light and in him is no darkness at all."

Everywhere, in heaven, there was glory, might and power, especially closer to the throne. Flowing from beneath the throne was the River of Life and it looked like a sea of glass and was, oh, so beautiful. This river sparkled like a clean cut diamond.

Revelation 22: 1 says, "And he showed me a pure river of water of life, clear as crystal, proceeding from the throne of God and of the Lamb."

My guiding angel appeared by my side and said, 'Come and see the glory of God.'

Very rapidly I was taken to a place that seemed to grow in intensity and volume with the high praises of God. Shouting, praising and sounds of joy were everywhere with a harmonious blend and it was like nothing I had ever heard.

Psalms 98:4: "Make a joyful noise unto the Lord..."

Psalms 47: 1: "...shout unto God..."

the angel of the Lord said, 'We are approaching the throne of God. How glorious, how beautiful this sight was.

WHEN GOD SPEAKS

TANDING IN FRONT OF the throne were twelve very large angels and they appeared to be over twelve feet tall and they were blowing their horns as God spoke.

The garments the angels wore were adorned with beautiful jewels. With the things they do and say the angels influence the atmosphere with music. The angels prepared the way for the Lord to speak with the things they did.

When the Lord spoke a thick cloud enveloped the mighty throne.

Revelation 4: 5: "And from the throne preceded lightning, thundering and voices. Seven lamps of fire were burning before the throne, which are the seven Spirits of God.

Power would follow from the front of the throne.

I listened as God spoke and his voice sounded like many waters.

Revelation 14: 2: "And I heard a voice from heaven, as the voice of many waters…"

Even though the voice was like many waters I understood every word that was said.

God spoke of His son's blood and how Christ blood was shed for all the people on the earth and how the blood of Christ could cleanse us from all our sins.

1 John 1: 7: "...the blood of Jesus Christ cleanseth us from all sin."

God extended this invitation to all who would listen.

Revelation 22: 17: "...whoever is thirsty come, whoever wishes may have the water of life as a free gift."

God said that His Son's blood was shed to redeem men and women from their sins. He said that putting His Son on the cross to give us eternal life was worth everything and that His Son's blood had paid the price to redeem us.

Ephesians 1: 7: "In Him we have redemption through his blood, the forgiveness of sins, according to the riches of his grace."

Colossians 1: 14: "In whom we have redemption through this blood, even the forgiveness of sins."

Revelation 1: 5: "Jesus Christ...loved us and washed us from our sins in His own blood."

Also read 1 Peter 1: 19-20, Hebrews 9: 28, 1Timothy 1: 15 and Luke 22: 20.

During my time in heaven I was thrilled and excited to be able to hear the voice of God, his voice was like a mighty roar, but was pleasant to my ears. The mighty roar did not distract me from understanding what was being said.

OH, God, everything you have made is so beautiful. And to think you made it all for us. There is no way we can comprehend of the things God has prepared for us that love him.

1 Corinthians 2: 9: "...eye hath not seen nor ear heard, neither have entered into the heart of man, the things which God hath prepared for them that love him."

HEAVEN, A REAL PLACE

EING HERE IN HEAVEN brought me to the realization that heaven is real, along with the people and the angels. Everything is real.

In heaven everything is so beautiful and real. To think I will inherit all this mind boggling beauty. All I have to do is continue serving God.

Matthew 25: 34: "Come ye blessed of my Father, inherit the kingdom prepared for you…"

it is a joy for me to talk of God's magnificence and of heaven. With all my heart I thank God for the opportunity of serving him.

My heart is full of thankfulness that he saved my soul from a fire-burning hell.

Psalm 16: 10: "For thou wilt not leave my soul in hell…"

Revelation 20: 15: "And whosoever was not found written in the book of life was cast into the lake of fire."

I thank God that I am a born-again, blood washed child of the King and that Jesus Christ is my Lord.

Luke 19: 10: "For the Son of man is come to seek and to save that which is lost."

Hebrews 7: 25: "Wherefore he is able to save them to the uttermost that come unto God by him…"

Friends, family and all others if you are not born again, you need to get down on your knees and ask the Lord to forgive you from your sins.

John 3: 3: "Except a man be born again he cannot see the Kingdom of God."

It is imperative for all who are not born again to ask Jesus Christ to come into their heart, cleanse and save their soul.

Believe in your heart that Jesus Christ is the Son of God that he was sent to earth by his father that he was born of the virgin, Mary. Believe he is the Holy Son of God, sent to redeem us from hell. The most important thing is you must believe that Jesus paid the only ultimate acceptable sacrifice for your sins when he died on the cross.

Acts 22: 16: "…wash away thy sins, calling on the name of the Lord."

Psalms 38: 18: "…I will be sorry for my sins."

Sinners you must be sorry for your sins and be willing to change.

WHAT HAPPENS TO CHILDREN

W HEN JESUS WAS ON earth he spoke many times about children.

Here are some scriptures where Jesus spoke about children.

Matthew 19: 14: "Let the little children come unto me and do not forbid them, for of such is the kingdom of heaven."

Matthew 18: 3-4: "Verily I say unto you, Except ye be converted and become as little children ye shall not enter unto the kingdom of heaven. Whosoever therefore shall humble himself as a child, the same is the greatest in the kingdom of heaven."

Luke 18: 16: "suffer little children to come unto me and forbid them not, for of such is the kingdom of God."

Mark 10: 15: "Whosoever shall not receive the kingdom of God as little child, he shall not enter therein."

Mark 9: 37: "Whosoever shall receive one of such children in my name, receiveth me and whosoever shall receive me receiveth not me, but him that sent me."

There is at least one scripture in the Old Testament.

Joel 1: 3: "Tell ye your children of it and let your children tell their children and their children another generation."

The people were going to have a shivering, exciting feeling concerning the children in this part of heaven.

My angel who had rainbow colored and triangle shaped wings was by my side. He wore a sparkling white robe and his hair was spun like pure, fine gold. Light and power enveloped him and his features were beautiful and glorious. My eyes were drawn to him because this was a sight I had never seen before.

He said to me; 'Come and see the glory of God. I am to show you the place where children go and what happens to them when they die.'

There is something I want to make completely clear. ***THERE ARE NO CHILDREN OR INFANTS IN HELL.*** I know this because when God allowed me to journey to hell there was not a single infant or child there.

I know that many will not agree with this explanation but it does not matter. For I know what the angel of the Lord showed me about heaven, hell and the place where children go when they die. I was ask to share this.

I praised God as I traveled with the angel. Higher and higher into the atmosphere we traveled and when we stopped the angel told me that he must show me these things.

REMEMBERING

S O MANY THINGS OCCURRED while I was on my journey with the angel. Some I cannot remember because I was not allowed to. While on my trip to heaven I was shown many events, some I remember and some I don't. But the things I do remember are enough to motivate me to tell all who will listen about heaven. In the book of Daniel it tells us that Daniel had complete understanding of his visions and dreams.

Daniel 10: 7: "Daniel alone saw the vision…"

When the Lord took me to heaven there was an overabundance of glory and power. Things went on that were not explained to me, certain parts of heaven, I did not see. The most exciting and wonderful part was where the infants and little children were.

UNBORN BABIES

I WAS TOLD BY THE angel of God to come and see. With a wave of his hand we were at a hospital maternity ward. Inside the labor room was a woman having a baby.

The angel told me that this woman was having a miscarriage. The mother was only three months along in her pregnancy.

Job 3: 16: "...as infants which never saw light?"

As I watched two beautiful appeared at the woman's bedside and in their hands they held something that looked like a basket which reminded me of a casket. This basket was made of white marbles and pearls, was closed on the sides and the lid opened on top. The basket was so stunning that I stood there staring at it for nothing could compare with it.

I could hear the angels praising God. The moment the woman had the miscarriage, the baby spirit, like a vapor arose from the tiny baby. Ever so gently the angels of God caught the baby's spirit, put it in the basket and immediately closed the lid, then raised their hands to heaven. Shouts of praise came from the angels. They acclaimed. 'To God be the Glory.' The angels acclaimed him and praised him highly as King of Kings and Lord of Lords and creator of all things in heaven and earth.

As the two angels passed in front of us they told us to come and see.

The four of us went back through the gate into heaven. This gate opened into a very beautiful part of heaven. This part was one I hadn't seen before nor had I gone through this entrance.

With my accompanying angel we went to another place of heaven. We flew upward, so high, I could see the throne and all around the throne I could hear the shouts and praises of God.

Ezra 3: 11: "With praise and thanksgiving, they sang to the Lord."

We approached from the left side of the throne. As we approached the throne I thought 'Oh! God, how beautiful and wonderful you are.' From every directions there was high praises to God.

Here are some examples of the Holy Scriptures that talk about angels.

Psalms 103: 20: "Bless the Lord, you his angels, who excel in strength, that do his commandments, hearkening unto the voice of his word."

Psalms 34: 7: "The angel of the Lord encampeth round about them that fear him and delivereth them."

Matthew 28: 2-3: "And behold, there was a great earthquake; for the angel of the Lord descended from heaven and came and rolled back the stone from the door, and sat upon it. His countenance was like lightning and his raiment white as snow."

There is a scripture where Jesus talks of someone being carried by the angels to heaven. I'm sure you are all familiar with the story of the beggar and the rich man.

Luke 16: 22: "And it came to pass, that the beggar died and was carried by the angels into Abraham's bosom, the rich man died and was buried."

ANGELS OF GOD

*I*N THE SCRIPTURES THERE are many references to angels. From the beginning of the Bible to the end there are numerous mentions of angels. It just goes to prove things over and over. It sheds light on it when someone is given a revelation.

Dreams, visions and revelation are my primary calling from God. I am a handmaiden of God and I love to tell this account concerning the children.

I was awed by what I saw and the voices of praise we heard. Surrounding the throne was thunder, lightning and the most beautiful rainbow that had ever been seen before. Covering the throne was an image of a man inside the cloud of glory.

The two angels that had been with the woman when she miscarried now set the basket; they had brought back to heaven with the baby's spirit, laid the basket on the throne and bowed. As they bowed their wings, shouts of Praise God, Glory and Hallelujah sounded all over heaven.

It felt like we were in an extremely large arena. In the midst were large angels blowing trumpets as if they were announcing something.

I did not see God.

John 1: 18: "No man hath seen God at anytime..."

Even though I did not see God, I seen the similarity of God as Moses did.

Exodus 33: 20: "but you cannot see my face because no one can see me and live."

I saw what was an image of God's hand open the basket. The hand came out of the cloud and opened the basket. Ever so softly and carefully the hand lifted the little soul out of the basket and laid it on the altar. The hands from the cloud begin to work on the little soul. The most perfect, beautiful form of young lady appeared as they finished their task. This sight that I beheld was awe-inspiring and it brought tears to my eyes.

My precious saints if you could only see the glory and power of God as I did. This power was wonderful, dazzling and beautiful.

IN GOD'S CARE

*O*N HEAVEN THERE WILL be no marks or blemishes.

Genesis 1: 27: "So God created man in his own image…"

I was told by the Lord that there will be no imperfections in heaven. Everything that was lost by the first Adam was restored by the second Adam.

The only sign of sin, in heaven, will be the scars in Jesus hands, feet and side. These scars will be a reminder that our blessed Lord paid the ultimate price for our redemption forever and ever.

I observed what I thought was the top of God's head.

Revelation 1: 14: "His head and hair were white as wool, as white as snow…"

As God breathed into the little soul, an extraordinary transformation took place and the soul became a fully perfect creation.

Harmoniously, the angels shouted and praised God. Watching this powerful manifestation of God's power, all the questions I ever had about infants, babies and children completely disappeared. Now, there are no doubts, in my mind, what happens to children after they die. I know they are in the hands of God, being made into perfection.

After witnessing this incredible transformation, my guardian angel and I went to a different place in heaven. In this place were beautiful trees with all kinds of fruits on them. Not only were there fruit tree but the ground was covered with flowers of every description. Birds of every color, shape and size were in this place. There is only word in my mind that describes heaven is; *indescribable!*

We journeyed to another place in heaven and here there were shouts of glory.

Revelation 5: 12: "Saying with a loud voice, Worthy is the Lamb that was slain to receive power and riches and wisdom and strength and honour and glory and blessing."

As we came upon a gate there was an angel standing there wearing a long, shimmering white robe and was sitting behind a desk. From his desk he picked a golden book and handed it to another angel.

After the angel received the book he opened it and rays of magnificent, sparkling light issued from it and begin to flash. This sight reminded me of millions of fireworks going off at the same time.

Before me parents and family members began to move and gravitate toward certain individuals. I could not understand what was taking place because people were jumping, leaping and shouting.

I turned to my guardian angel and ask about this scene.

The angel explained to me that these were loved ones recognizing their family members. He went on to say that these people are those who had been dismembered, paralyzed, crippled or who had died prematurely. Now by the power of God they were made whole and in a state of highest excellence.

There will be no strangers in heaven, for we will know everyone. Jacob, Isaac, Abraham, Moses and all the other prophets will be known to us. The disciples of Jesus, in the New Testament, will also be known to us.

Every person in heaven will be known to us and you will know just as God knows you.

1 Corinthians 13: 12: "For now we see through a glass darkly; but then face to face; now I know in part, but then shall I know even as also I am known."

The Everyday Bible states it this way. "Now we see a dim reflection, as if we were looking into a mirror, but then we shall see clearly. Now I now a part, but then will know fully, as God has known me."

In heaven we will have extensive knowledge.

'Come, we are going through this gate.' I was told by the angel.

So far, this was the most beautiful gate I had seen in heaven. This gate reminded me of a garden gate, but was far more beautiful. A garden gate was generally made out of wood, but this gate was made of the purest white stone or marble. Around this gate grew the most beautiful flowers. I stood admiring these flowers until the angel bade me to come. We entered through the gate and what I heard was beyond word, for in this part of heaven there was great rejoicing because of the reunion of all God's family.

A HEAVENLY REUNION

King David knew that when a baby or little children die their soul will go to heaven, where one day they will be reunited with their believing families. King David had a son who had been conceived out of wedlock in an adulterous affair with Bathsheba. Because of this the son died. After the death of his son, King David repented of his sin and was certain God had forgiven him.

In Psalms 32: 5 David said; "Then I confessed my sins to you and didn't hide my guilt. I will confess my sins to the Lord and you forgave my guilt."

David found peace in the knowledge that he would spend eternity in heaven with God.

Psalms 23: 6: "…and I will live in the house of the Lord forever."

He knew he would be reunited with his son, in heaven. With the assurance that they would see their son one day David was able to comfort Bathsheba.

2 Samuel 12:23: "But now that the baby is dead, why should I go without food? I can't bring him back

to life. Someday, I will go to him, but he cannot come back to me."

2 Samuel 12: 13-14 and 16-24 gives us an account of this incident. "Then David said to Nathan, I have sinned against the Lord. Nathan answered, 'The Lord has taken away your sin, you will not die. But what you did caused the Lord's enemies to lose all respect for him. For this reason the son who was born to you will die. David prayed to God to God for the baby. He refused to eat or drink. He went into his house and stayed there, lying on the ground all night. The older leaders of David's family came to him and tried to pull him up from the ground, but he refused to get up or to eat food with them. On the seventh day the baby died, David's servants were afraid to tell him that the baby was dead…Then David saw his servants whispering, he knew the baby was dead. So he ask them, 'Is the baby dead? They answered, he is dead.'

Then David got up from the floor, washed himself, put on lotion and changed his clothes. Then he went into the Lord's house to worship. After that, he went home and ask for something to eat. His servants gave him food and he ate.

David's servants said to him, 'Why are you doing this? When the baby was still alive, you refused to eat and you cried. Now that the baby is dead, you get up and eat food. David said 'While the baby was still alive, I refused to eat and I cried. I thought 'Who knows'? Maybe the Lord will feel sorry for me and let the baby live. But now that the baby is dead, why should I go without food? I can't bring him back to life. Someday I will go to him, but he cannot come to me. Then David comforted Bathsheba."

The angel of the Lord said there was one important thing he wanted me to know. From the moment of conception, a baby is an eternal soul. Whether a baby dies naturally or is aborted God knows about it. Over the precious small souls God has given angels charge over them.

The little souls are brought to heaven by angels. Once in heaven God completes them. Whether the baby dies naturally or is aborted, it doesn't matter because by the mighty hand of God the baby or child are formed and fashioned into perfection.

Deuteronomy 32: 4: "...his work is perfect..."

In order for parents to see their children who have gone on to heaven they must live righteously in Christ Jesus. If they do this, when they go to heaven, they will be reunited with and well know their precious loved ones. The gates of glory will be their meeting place.

WORSHIPPING AROUND THE THRONE

I AM OVERJOYED THAT THE Lord has given me the opportunity to share this vision. Every day it burns my heart continually. At first I wanted to keep this unique experience to myself and a few friends but they encouraged me to write down this testimony and to share the vision God had given me.

My dear people, I want you to know heaven is real—so I still have more to share with you.

Acts 7: 49 tells us that heaven is Jesus throne. Your loved ones, who have gone on before you, will meet you at the gates of glory. We have a blessed hope in Christ Jesus if only we believe—so be encouraged.

Colossians 2: 7: "…Christ in you, the hope of glory."

Jesus died on the cross for us and arose on the third day. He was lifted up to prepare us a place in heaven.

In John 14: 2: Jesus tells us, "In my Father's house are many mansions. If it were not so, I would have told you. I go to prepare a place for you."

I was surprised to see how large and mighty the angels were. The robes they wore sparkled, shimmered and radiated extremely large amounts of light. These angels were powerful and genuine with their minds set to glorify God. At every pearl gate in heaven there was an angel posted. By their sides these protecting angels wore swords.

Hallelujah, Glory to God. God surely protects his children.

THE ANGELS OF GOD

THE HOLY BIBLE IS full of scriptures that refer to angels.

I am greatly surprised that at one time or another we are inclined to overlook things that prove God's word over and over. Light is shed on the subject when a revelation is given to someone.

I will list a few of the scriptures that refer to angels.

Luke 15: 10: "...there is joy in the presence of the angels of God over one sinner that repenteth."

Hebrews 1: 14: "Are they not all ministering spirits, sent forth to minister to them who shall be heirs of salvation?"

Luke 22: 43: "And there appeared an angel unto him from heaven, strengthening him."

Genesis 24: 40: "...the Lord, before whom I walk, will send his angel with thee and prosper thy ways."

Psalms 91: 11-12: "For he shall give his angels charge over thee, to keep thee in all thy ways. They shall bear thee up in their hands, lest thou dash thy foot against a stone."

Mark 12: 25: "For when they shall rise from the dead, they neither marry, nor are given in marriages, but are as the angels which are in heaven."

Mark 1: 13: "...the angels ministered unto him."

Revelation 18: 1: "...I saw another mighty angel come down from heaven, having great power and the earth was lightened with his glory."

Revelation 10: 1: "And I saw another mighty angel come down from heaven, clothed with a cloud: and a rainbow was upon his head and his face was as it were the sun and his feet as pillars of fire."

These are but a few of the scriptures talking about angels. As you read and study God's holy word you will find many more references on angels. As you read your heart will be uplifted. I can guarantee that.

In heaven there will be no diseases, disabilities, wheelchairs or sickness, for we will be changed in a twinkling of an eye.

1 Corinthians 15: 52: "...in the twinkling of an eye...we shall be changed."

As I re-entered the gate of heaven, I was overcome completely with the joy and peace that was there. Glorious singing and praises filled the air. The peace in heaven is indescribable because there is nothing on earth that can compare with it. The beings on earth have never felt peace like this. Heaven is perfect and beautiful with no corruption. No lies, no sin because God will not allow a single sin to enter through the pearly gates of heaven. John 13: 24: "Strive to enter in at the strait gate; for many I say unto you, will seek to enter in and shall not be able."

Matthew 7: 13-14: "Enter ye in at the strait gate; for wide is the gate and broad is the way that leadeth to destruction and many there be which go in there at. Because strait is the gate and narrow is the way which leadeth unto life and few there be that find it."

Since the first sin in the Garden of Eden the people on earth have never experienced the joy, peace and rest that heaven has.

THE GRAND SPECTACULAR

QUICKLY THE ANGEL GUIDED me over to the River of Life. There along the banks were many different fruit trees and every one of them was loaded with fruit.

Genesis 1: 11: "And God said, Let the earth bring forth... fruit trees yielding fruit after its kind..."

As we moved along it felt like we became part of the music. Wherever we went in heaven there was music and it was always new. The continuous musical praises were lifted up in honor and praise to God.

The angel said to me; 'We are going before the throne to see the worship of God.' As we traveled towards the throne of God, a great multitude of people came from all over heaven. All these people were coming to the throne to worship the King of Kings and the Lord of Lords.

WORSHIP IN HEAVEN

S WE TRAVELED ON more and more people joined the group. Soon there were so many coming that they could not be counted. From every corner of heaven they came. It was plain to see we were going to a huge arena-type area.

John described this in Revelation 4: 2-5 and 10-11. "Immediately I was in the spirit and before me was a throne in heaven and someone was sitting on it. The One who sat on the throne looked like precious stones, like jasper and carnelian. All around the throne was a rainbow the color of an emerald. Around the throne there were twenty-four other thrones with twenty-four elders sitting on them. They were dressed in white and had golden crowns on their heads. Lightning flashes and noises and thundering came from the throne. Before the throne seven lamps were burning, which are the seven spirits of God. Then the twenty-four elders bow down before the One who sits on the throne and they worship him who lives forever and ever. They put their crowns down before the throne and say: You are worthy, our Lord and God, to receive glory and honor and power, because you made all things. Everything existed and was made because you wanted it."

In and around the throne the most beautiful clouds rolled. These clouds were shaped like mushrooms and were mixed with beautiful colors and glory. Above the clouds and throne was a beautiful rainbow. The intensity of God is hard to imagine.

There was no doubt in my mind that the image of the man I saw in the clouds was the likeness of God.

God wanted to make man in his own image and he did it.

Genesis 1: 27: "So God created man in his own image, in the image of God created he him, male and female created he them."

Out of the dust of the ground God made man. Just think about the power of God that must have been present.

Genesis 2: 7: "And the Lord God formed man out of the dust of the ground and breathed into his nostrils the breath of life and man became a living soul."

Adam was alone at first so God made a companion for him.

Genesis 2: 20: "So God put Adam, removed a rib and fashioned woman from it."

Genesis 2: 21-22: "And the Lord God caused a deep sleep to fall upon Adam and he slept; and he took one of his ribs and closed up the flesh instead thereof. And the rib, which the Lord God had taken from man, made he a woman and brought her unto the man."

Eve was also made in the image of God. She was to be Adams lifelong companion and mate. What glory was given to human beings to be made in the image of God?

PREPARE FOR THE KING

THE BEAUTY AND HOLINESS of God were shown by testimonies of worship. People and angels were everywhere in this meeting place. Never was there any chaos for everything was done in an orderly manner. Everywhere and I mean everywhere people and angels praised God.

From the throne of God flowed the River of Life. Even though it seemed like a sea of glass or crystal, it still was flowing.

Looking around I seen horses.

Revelation 6: 2: "And I saw and behold a white horse…"

These gorgeous, magnificent horses looked like they had been chiseled from marble. But saints, these were physically real horses. They were so beautiful that not one single flaw could be found. All the horses were elegant and each one of them had white blankets upon their backs, neatly trimmed in gold. In their mouth were golden reins and on their feet were ornaments, which extended to their tails. As they stood around the throne the horses were very watchful.

There were twelve angels which held trumpets and musical horns by their sides as they stood before the throne. The robes they wore flowed gracefully and each robe was trimmed in gold with large rubies and other immense stones embedded within them.

Other musical instruments suddenly appeared and these instruments were spectacular. Never in my life did I imagine I would behold anything like these instruments. Harps were numerous. In order to see who was stationed at these instruments, I looked around.

Glory to God---Hallelujah—Glory, Glory!!

CHILDREN

As I LOOKED AROUND I realized God has with him, in heaven, some of the things he created on earth. Lush, beautiful valleys, lots of mountains and streams of water. You know saints, I even seen snow, but none of the cold associated with it.

The flowers in heaven were some I had never seen in my life and the fragrance was beyond my imagination. The smell was sweet and fragrant. The colors were magnificent and these colors were nothing like the colors on earth. Every color imaginable could be seen. The gold was as transparent as crystal but still looked like gold.

For some reason I thought there was only grown-ups in heaven, but there were children there also. Horses, dogs and large cats like lion were there.

Every person, angel and animal was headed towards the throne of God, which I could see in a distance. God's throne was high and lifted up, so it could be seen from every direction.

Revelation 4: 2: "…behold a throne was set in heaven and one sat on the throne."

While carrying harps, children sang and praised God.

'Now what are these children doing here?

The religious truths concerning children being in heaven was explained to me.

'Where did all these children come from,' I ask my angel. His answer to me was that these children were children the earth did not want and that they were brought to heaven by God.

I answered him by saying that I thought people went to heaven because they chose to.

'Children must be taught the oracles of God.'

There were many, many teachers and angels performing the task of teaching the children about God.

'Are you talking about abortions?' I ask.

'Yes, these are children waiting to see their mothers.'

The children I seen in this area seemed to be between three and ten. The younger children and babies were in another area.

On their harps the children played beautiful songs as they sung with the other people and there was a lot of shouting and joy for everyone was excited. Whispering swirled around me and these whispers were that; He's coming, he's coming.

'Who's coming? I ask the angel.

'You shall see the Holy One.' He answered.

Coming from the city I saw a light approaching. It was still a long way off but the children ran towards this light. As I seen the children's reaction I knew this must be Jesus.

As of yet I was too far off to see the face of Jesus, but I could see his hand reaching out to the children as they played, sang and hugged him. Every single one of the children adored the Lord.

Mark 10: 14: "Suffer the little children to come unto me...for of such is the kingdom of God."

MANY DIFFERENT RACES

*O*N HEAVEN I SAW many different races. One group of Oriental children caught my eye. They were being taught the oracles of God by one of the heavenly ladies.

I ask if the parents of the children were there.

'Some are, but most of them are not. Once they come to the age of accountability they have a choose whether to accept or reject God. Even though the parents may reject God and go the other way, God is merciful and doesn't reject their children. A good number of children pass away at an early age, so we teach them and they grow.'

My younger sister lost a baby, when she was less than two years old and I am sure she will see her daughter in heaven. Beautiful and free from imperfections. Her child will be taught the oracles of God.

WITHIN HEAVEN'S GATE

I LEARNED THAT HEAVEN PARTIALLY consists of those things which make us the happiest on earth, wonderfully glorified by the presence of the Master. My vision is not everyone's vision and if any of these scenes portrayed seem irreverent in view of our Christian training, I can only say: 'This is the way it came to me.' I pray this vision will give hope, comfort and uplift all who read it.

I was greatly surprised to see books in heaven.

'Why are these books in heaven?' I ask.

My angels reply to me was; 'Why not? The mortals have strange ideas of the pleasures and duties of this blessed life. They seem to think that death of the body means an entire change to the soul. But I want you to know, this is not the case, by any means. The same tastes, desires and knowledge we had before death we take to heaven.

I pray I can make you all understand that we are building for eternity during our earthly life. Our purest thoughts, our distinguished ambitions, our exalted aspirations, our highest rank are taken among the host of heaven. We must follow the studies and duties, earnestly in our life of probation, so we will be better prepared to carry them forward, toward completion and perfection.

THE SEA

MY GUARDIAN ANGEL AND I went on a special journey to the sea which was filled with holy joy. I stood motionless and mute before the overwhelming glory of the scene before me. Sloping downward the scene was a golden beach. Like the dust of diamonds and other precious stones the beach caught and radiated the light until it sparkled and glimmered.

The waves as they came and went caught up this sparkling sand and carried it out on their crests.

'The Sea! The Sea!' the sea spread out before us in a vivid brightness which exceeds description in any language.

Upon the sea, in every direction, there were boats representing every nation and nothing on earth could compare to the beauty of these boats. These boats looked like great, open pleasure barges and these were filled with people looking toward the shore.

There were people as far as I could see on the shore and they were numberless as the sand on the sea. As far as the eye could see a great mass of beautiful souls clothed in spotless garments of the redeemed stood. Many of these had golden harps and other various musical instruments. As each passenger came ashore they were welcomed by affectionate embraces and happy voices of their loved ones. The harps were held high and all the golden instruments would sound and the immense crowd broke forth into a triumphant song of victory over death and the grave.

1 Corinthians 15: 55: "O death, where is thy sting? O grave where is thy victory?"

'Do these people always stand here?' I ask.

A radiant being near me said; 'Not the same people. BUT! There is always a crowd of people here looking forward to friends and loved ones from the other side and those who gather together to share in joy. A number of the heavenly choristers are always here, but not always the same ones.

The radiant one walked towards the shore and left me enfolded in wonder and awe. I was enraptured in watching the reunions and found myself joining with interest in the happy songs of rejoicing.

There was one boat of beauty and extraordinary strength that gracefully floated over the waves. Near the front of the boat was a handsome man with his arms around a very graceful woman. Both the man and woman shielded their eyes against the rare brilliant light. They scanned and searched the faces of the crowd yearning to see their loved ones.

A great thrill of joy surged through my body because the couple I seen was my precious daughter and her husband.

Instantly I was moving swiftly through the crowd towards the boat. As soon as the boat touched the shore my precious daughter and her husband came running towards me. It was a rapturous moment as we embrace each other. My life in heaven was now complete and there would never be anymore parting. The heavenly choir broke into song as I stood embracing my daughter and son-in-law, scarcely realizing the unexpected bliss. With uplifted faces shining with joy, our eyes filled with happy tears, our voices trembled with emotion and the three of us joined in this glad song of praise.

"Glory be unto the Father and the Son!

Glory be unto the ever-blessed three in one.

No more sorrow, no more parting, no grief or pain.

Christ has broken death's strong fetters and we are free again.

Alleluia! Amen!

GLIMPSE OF ETERNITY

*A*BOUT FOUR AM. My body functions stopped much as they had once earlier. Being this early in the morning there was no one around to call for emergency help.

The transition was peaceful and serene. I found myself walking up a beautiful green hill but it seemed like my leg movements were effortless and a deep ecstasy flooded my body. I stood on this hill free from pain. Looking down my body seemed to be a blur and colorless. The grass I was walking on was the most vivid shade of green. Each blade was vibrating and moving and had the texture of fine velvet. As my feet touched the ground something was transmitted through my body.

I ask myself, 'Can this be death?' If it was I certainly had nothing to fear. Here there was no darkness and no uncertainty, only a total sense of well being and a change in location.

Light was everywhere even without the sun. As I walked along I saw multicolored flowers, trees and shrubs.

As traveled along I came upon a beautiful, silver structure which reminded me of a palace. I could hear voices as I came near this structure. These voices melodiously and harmoniously blended in chorus singing the praises of Jesus and there were several parts to their harmony. I joined in as I heard and felt the singing. After for awhile the music softened and new choruses were picked up by unseen voices. I was surprised because these voices had more than four parts and were singing in different languages. There was a richness and perfect blending of the words and I was surprised I understood every word.

An angel told me that wherever we willed ourselves to go, we would be there instantly.

Going a few steps ahead of me, the angel put his hand on a gate which I hadn't noticed before. This gate seemed to be twelve feet high and was made of solid sheets of pearl with no handle. The scroll work at the top of his Gothic structure caught my attention. This gate of pearl was so translucent that I could almost see through it. At the thought that I would be able to go inside excited me. Taking a step forward the angel placed his hand upon the gate and miraculously an opening appeared in the center of the pearl panel. This opening widened and deepened as though the material was dissolving. I was overcome by the brightness of the gold that covered the streets. I was conscious of a person even though no figure was visible. Immediately I knew that this brightness was Jesus—the person was Jesus. Suddenly I felt bathed by rays of a powerful, penetrating and loving energy.

CALL TO WORSHIP

THE HOLY SPIRIT SHOWED me something. In the center of a group of horses, a woman stood still. The angels in front of the throne picked up their trumpets and horns, which were at their sides, and began blowing. The sounds of high praise and joy went up as the angels blew their instruments.

From somewhere, in heaven, I heard a loud voice proclaim; 'It is now time to worship the King of Kings and Lord of Lords for his glorious acts and his glorious power unto the people of the earth.'

1 Timothy 6: 15: "...the King of Kings and Lord of Lords."

This voice from heaven continued speaking and said; "Give God high praise and worship him in song and dance, worship him with music and worship him for his goodness."

Psalms 98: 4-6: "Make a joyful noise unto the Lord all the earth, make a loud noise and rejoice and sing praise. Sing unto the Lord with the harp...with trumpets and sound of cornet make a joyful noise unto the Lord."

The voice continued with the statement the 'He is God, the King of Kings and he is the redeemer of mankind.'

Psalms 19: 14: "…O Lord, my strength and my redeemer."

As the announcer spoke the trumpets sounded. There was an angel reading a scroll, she stopped and a signal was given.

The magnificent horses bowed to their knees as the signal was given. All in a row, their heads went down in praise to the name of the Lord.

Philippians 12:10: "That at the name of Jesus every knee should bow…"

Revelation 5: 13: "Then I heard all creatures in heaven and on earth and under the earth and in the sea. To the one who sits on the throne and to the Lamb be praise and honor and glory and power forever and ever."

Before the Lord the horses began to spin and prance. These horses did all kinds of things to magnify, praise and worship God.

PEOPLE!! If only you could have seen this and seen how pleased God was with the worship unto him.

MOTIVATION TO PRAISE

SAINTS, DO YOU REALIZE how much God loves you? God wants us to praise him, even when we are going through sorrows or heartaches.

Psalms 34: 18: "The Lord is nigh unto them that are of a broken heart…"

Saints, we are to praise God, not because of trials or sorrows, but because we love him.

Not for our sake but for the sake of God we should worship him. We shift our focus from ourselves to God as we praise him for the mighty things he has done for us. As we enter into worship we come to understand clearly that God is the one who can solve the problems we are facing and that we can trust him to come to our aid. When we truly praise and worship the Lord we benefit from it.

Psalm 68: 19: "Blessed be the Lord who daily loadeth us with benefits…"

ACCOLADES (HONOR-PRAISE)
OF PRAISE

I COULD HEAR THE HEAVENLY musicians playing as other worshippers came in. thousands and thousands sang in honor and praise to God. Glorious shouting could be heard, along with the singing that covered heaven all the glorious singing, shouting and praising went on for a long time.

I can never explain how beautiful it is to hear and be in the midst of praises to God.

In the center of the echoing, splendid sounds, the earth seemed so far away, along with the troubles and sorrows. Even the horrors of hell, that I had experienced earlier, seemed very far away.

MY ASSIGNMENT FROM GOD

EEP WITHIN MY HEART I knew there was something the Lord wanted me to do. The angel of God touched my shoulder and strength came rushing through my body.

I was told by the angel of God that I had been allowed to see and experience the things I did so I would be able to share, tell and record them. 'These revelations, visions and dreams have been given to you to let people, on earth, know the things which God has prepared for those who love him.'

1 Corinthians 2: 9: "…eye hath not seen, nor ear heard, neither have entered into the heart of man, the things which God has prepared for them that love him."

Deuteronomy 7: 9: "…that love him and keep his commandments…"

God spoke to me and the sound of his voice filled me with ecstasy. I understood every word, even though it sounded like thunder. I was so overwhelmed that I fell on my face and began to praise and worship the King of Kings and Lord of Lords.

HEAVENLY SCRIPTURES

*A*FTER I RETURNED TO earth I pondered the many things God had shown me. I found myself absorbed in the Word of God. There are many verses about heaven and God's majesty.

Here are a few:

Hebrews 12: 22: "But ye are come unto Mount Sion and unto the city of the living God, the heavenly Jerusalem, and to an innumerable company of angels."

Job 22: 12 and 14: "Is not God in the height of heaven? Thick clouds are a covering to him that he seeth not; and he walketh in the circuit of heaven.

Nehemiah 9: 6: "Thou, even thou, art Lord alone; thou hast made heaven, the heaven of heavens, with all their host, the earth and all that is herein and thou perserveth them all; and the host of heaven worshippeth thee."

Psalm 102: 19:

"For He hath looked down from the height of his sanctuary; from heaven did the Lord behold the earth."

Psalm 103: 19: "The Lord hath prepared his throne in the heavens and his kingdom ruleth over all."

Psalm 148: 13: "Let them praise the name of the Lord: for his name alone is excellent; his glory is above the earth and heaven."

HOLY CREATURES IN HEAVEN

THE ANGEL OF THE Lord said to me; 'Behold the Glory of God.'

Through one of the many gates of heaven I was taken. Each and every gate was made of exquisite pearls with designs engraved and was so beautiful I could never describe them. *Heaven is so beautiful!!!* On the River of Life people stood shouting and praising God. While this was happening the angel took me before the throne of God.

Revelation 4: 2: "…a throne was set in heaven and one sat on the throne."

Oh! The shouts and worship.

Saints! I was given the privilege of seeing the throne of God. Surrounding the throne is an exquisite rainbow. Even though the rainbow was beautiful it was overshadowed with a cloud of glory and the brilliance of the power of God. Also surrounding the throne was voices, lightning and thunder and I was blessed to see the divine manifestations of God.

Revelation 4: 5-6: "Lightning flashes and noises and thunder came from the throne. Before the throne seven lamps were burning, which are the seven spirits of God."

Also before the throne there were four living creatures with eyes all over them, in front and back. Around the throne I heard the multiplied voices of angels. The number of angels could not be estimated. I saw the heavenly creatures and the elders. There were four of the heavenly creatures and twenty-four elders.

Revelation 5: 11: "Then I looked and I heard the voices of many angels around the throne and the four living creatures and the elders. There were thousands and thousands of angels.

Revelation 7: 11: "All the angels were standing around the throne and the elders and the four living creatures. They all bowed down on their faces before the throne and worshipped God."

THE LIVING CREATURES

EFORE THE THRONE OF God I saw the four living creatures. I knew about these creatures that were around the throne because I had read about them in the book of Revelation.

All these heavenly creatures had very large eyes, some in the front and some in the back. They could see in front of them as well as in the back of them. The stature of these heavenly creatures was very large. I had seen tall people on earth but nothing like these creatures.

Each of the creatures had six wings. One creature had the face of a lion, the second had a face like a calf, the third had a face of a man, and the fourth had a face like a flying eagle. Can you imagine a creature that is very tall with six wings?

The chant of 'Holy, Holy, Holy, Lord God Almighty' was cried constantly by these creatures.

These creatures looked strange to me because I had never seen anything that resembled them in appearance but I knew God had made everything on earth and in heaven, so these were his creation. God is an awesome God and I praise him for his mighty acts and power. As I watched the heavenly creatures continually worshipped God.

These creatures confused me so when I returned to earth I studied the book of Revelation and found what I was looking for.

Revelation 4: 6-8: "Also there before the throne there was something that looked like a sea of glass, clear as crystals. In the center and around the throne were four living creatures with eyes all over them, in front and back. The first living creature was like a lion, the second was like a calf, the third had a face of a man, the fourth was like a flying eagle. Each of these four living creatures had six wings and was covered all over with eyes, inside and out. Day and night they never stopped saying: 'Holy, Holy, Holy is the Lord God Almighty."

He was, he is and he is coming.

THE DUTIES OF THE LIVING CREATURES

EADING THE SCRIPTURES I saw where God told us about these living creatures and their duties. One of their duties was to continually give God praise and honor. Along with the twenty-four elders worshipping God was the heavenly creatures' occupation.

Here are some scriptures in Revelation that will help you understand the duties of the creatures and elders.

Revelation 4: 8-11: "Each of these four living creatures had six wings and was covered all over with eyes, inside and out. Day and night they never stop saying; 'Holy, Holy, Holy, is the Lord God Almighty. He was, he is and he is coming. These living creatures give glory, honor and thanks to the one who sits on the throne and they worship him who lives forever and ever. They put their crowns down before the throne and say 'You are worthy, our Lord and God to receive glory and honor and power because you made all things. Everything existed and was made because you wanted it."

Revelation 5: 9-10: "And they all sang a new song to the Lamb. 'You are worthy to take the scroll and to open its seals because you were killed and with the blood of your death you bought people for God from every tribe, language, people and nations. You made them to a kingdom of priests for our God and they will rule on the earth."

Revelation 5: 11-14: "Then I looked and I heard the voices of many angels around the throne, and the four creatures and the elders. There were thousands and thousands of angels, saying in a loud voice, 'The Lamb who was killed is worthy to receive power, wealth, wisdom and strength, honor, glory and praise. Then I heard all creatures in heaven and on earth and under the earth and in the sea saying 'To the One who sits on the throne and to the Lamb be praise and honor and glory and power forever and ever. The four living creatures said 'Amen' and the elders bowed down and worshipped."

Revelation 7: 11-12: "All the angels were standing around the throne and the elders and the four living creatures. They all bowed down on their faces before the throne and worshipped God, saying 'Amen! Praise, glory and wisdom, thanks, honor, power and strength belong to our God forever and ever. Amen."

Revelation 19: 4-6: "Then the twenty-four elders and the four living creatures bowed down and worshipped God, who sits on the throne. They said,

'Amen, Hallelujah! Our Lord God, the Almighty rules."

There are others duties of the living creatures and they are found in Revelation 5: 8: "When he took the scroll, the four living creatures and twenty-four elders bowed down before the Lamb. Each one had a harp and a golden bowl full of incense, which are the prayers if God's holy people."

Revelation 6: 1: "Then I watched while the Lamb opened the first of seven seals. I heard one of the four living creatures say with a voice like thunder, 'Come!'

Revelation 15: 6-8: "And the seven angels bringing the seven disasters came out of the temple. They were dressed in clean, shining new linen and wore golden bands, tied around their chest. Then one of the four living creatures gave to the seven angels seven golden bowls filled with the anger of God, who lives forever and ever. The temple was filled with smoke from the glory and power of God and no one cloud could enter the temple until the seven disasters of the seven angels were finished."

THE GLORIES OF HEAVEN

*I*MMEDIATELY AFTER GOD SHOWED me hell he revealed heaven to me and by the power of God Almighty I was taken on numerous visits around the different parts of heaven.

I was fascinated with heaven because there is no sorrow, death, dying, or grief, only joy, peace, happiness and the fruits of the Spirit everywhere.

Also fascinating me were the thousands of angels. Some of them had wings and some did not. The angels were busy at all times and were never idle. The angels were performing tasks and taking care of details constantly. Each angel had their certain jobs and separate assignments to do. As they did their jobs they were praising God and performing their duties happily.

Colossians 3: 17: "And whatsoever ye do in word or deed, do all in the name of the Lord Jesus, giving thanks to God and the Father by him."

The Everyday Bible states it like this: "Everything you do or say should be done to obey Jesus your Lord. And in all you do, give thanks to God the Father."

Philippians 4: 4: "Rejoice in the Lord always and again I say 'rejoice.'

Constantly angels were occupied with their duties. One of the duties of the angels was to lead new souls through the River of Life. Then the angels would escort the new soul to a place where other angels would outfit them with gowns of salvation, which are robes of righteousness. The new soul is then taken by their angelic guide to a room of crowns, where that person is fitted with a crown.

Everything is done in a perfect, beautiful order. Every angel that was involved with these duties was perfectly happy doing them.

Bells were constantly ringing in heaven even though I never saw them. It was explained to me that each time the bell rang it meant a soul on earth was just saved. 'The Glories of Heaven' was what it was called.

HEAVENLY FURNISHINGS

I SAW BEAUTIFUL TABLES ON my trip to heaven and to describe them adequately, I could not do. On earth I had seen beautiful furniture, as most of you have, but nothing on earth could compare to these tables. The tables that were in heaven were exquisitely designed and made and had elaborate designs in them.

There were many other furnishings in heaven including an untold number of books.

HEAVENLY RECORDING

SAINTS!! I HAVE AN important message. Every time you help others in need, give money, pay tithes, or anything else you do for the glory of God is recorded in heaven. When the Lord showed me his mighty glories and powers, it left a lasting impression that will never be erased from my mind.

During my journey to heaven I saw angels constantly coming and going. Many of the angels were coming to heaven with reports from all over the earth. Each angel would go to a certain room with a recording angel that was in charge.

Reading the report was the messenger angel and the recording angel would ask, 'Are you a witness? Did you see this take place?' once the report was confirmed it was logged into a book. Eventually the report was sent to the throne of God. But first they had to go through a special process.

The Spirit of God was moving constantly in heaven and it was greater than anything on earth. Saints! Do you know that the things on earth are patterned after the things in heaven? The things on earth are only a shadowy reflection of those in heaven. The unbelievable music, the unhindered praises and other glories in heaven, can only be imagined by us mortals.

God wants people to praise Him. From the very first chapter of Genesis to the last chapter of Revelation, God expressed his desire for a family to love him.

Saints; remember that heaven is a place God has prepared for us that love him. As a child of God my home will be in heaven and if you are born again and have repented of your sins and have Jesus Christ in your heart, heaven will be your home also.

The Lord can wash away your sins through his precious blood.

John 1: 29: "...Behold the Lamb of God, which taketh away the sin of the world."

THE CLEANSING BLOOD

I WANT TO SHOW YOU another aspect of the records room, which I had described earlier. In certain sections of the record room sat a number of angels which had golden buckets in front of them. This is also a part of 'The Glories of Heaven.'

Not only did the angels have buckets in front of them, they had stacks of books. I learned in these books were messages from all over the earth. These messages had to be looked over carefully and closely by a recording angel.

A couple more angels brought messages from earth as I stood there watching. I was told these new messages were someone being born again and had been truly saved from their sins by accepting Jesus Christ into their hearts. When someone, on earth, truly repented of their sins and asks Jesus to be their Savior and Lord, it was recorded that the person had given his/ her life to the Lord.

From the stack each angel with golden buckets took a book and in their hands each angel held what looked like a bloodstained cloth. This bloodstained cloth was mixed with power, light and glory. It was beautiful—not gory or anything. With God's direction, each angel erased the old history of the sinner and recorded that he/she had been born again.

Isaiah 43: 25: "I even I, am he that blotteth out thy transgressions for mine own sake and will not remember thy sins."

Saints, the word of God is true and God truly forgives our sins. To see the angels wash the pages clean was very pleasing. Glory, Hallelujah! God wipes the slate clean for each and every one of us.

I could hear the saints singing this hymn:

"Nothing but the blood of Jesus can wash my sins away. Nothing but the blood of Jesus can make me whole today. Nothing but the blood of Jesus can cleanse me today."

Then the angels sang this song:

"Another one's been redeemed by the blood of the Lamb. Another one's been saved from the devil's hand by the blood of the Lamb. Another one has been saved from hell by the blood of Jesus Christ."

Saints, never be ashamed to call upon the power of the blood of Jesus Christ. His blood was shed on the cross for us over two thousand years ago to wash away our sins and it has never lost its power. Jesus went to the cross for us and conquered the devil.

Hebrews 7: 27: "…Christ offered his sacrifice only once and for all time when he offered himself."

Christ came down from glory and was born of a virgin. Jesus gave his life in order that we could be redeemed by his precious blood. He died on the cross so we would not have to go to hell, the awful place I was shown.

I want you all to know the Word of God is true. It thrilled my heart to see the angels wash away the history from the stacks of the books. The angels erased all the old past, the old sins and all the dirty things. Every single thing of the past was gone now because of the blood of Jesus had eradicated them all.

ALTARS OF GOD

I LOVE THE ALTARS OF God. Whenever I am in a spirit-filled church and see the beautiful altars, I know many tears have been shed on them.

Malachi 2: 13: "...you cover the Lord's altar with tears..."

Time after time, in the Old Testament, God repeatedly commanded his people to destroy the altars of the heathens, in every city they conquered.

Deuteronomy 12: 3-4: "Tear down the altars, smash their holy stone pillar and burn their Asherah idols in the fire, cut down their idols and destroy their names from those places. Don't worship the Lord your God that way."

God instructed his people to destroy completely and rid all the sinful altars that did not give praise to him. God's people were to remove the altars that did not honor or reverence him. After these were completely destroyed, they were to build and keep altars only to worship the Lord.

In Judges there are the instructions.

Only Jesus can do this for you, for you cannot do it yourself.

Judges 6: 25-26: "...Take the bull that belongs to your father and a second bull seven years old. Pull down your father's altar to Baal and cut down the Ashernah idol beside it. Then build an altar to the Lord God with its stones in the right order on this high ground. Kill and burn a second bull on this altar, using the wood from the Ashernah idol."

TODAY'S ALTARS

SAINTS, WHEN WE BOW down in front of an altar and pour our hearts out to God; it shows we are not ashamed of him.

We can be in the presence of God when we kneel at a dedicated altar, in front of the church. At this altar we can call on God, confess our sins and ask for his forgiveness.

1 John 1: 9: "If we confess our sins, he is faithful and just to forgive us our sins…"

When we are kneeling at a dedicated altar we can feel Gods awesome power. As we feel his power we are given the assurance he answers our prayers. Being in the presence of God we can feel his loving arms encircling us. The altars, the old-fashioned of God, in churches, are something wonderful. At these altars we can go and kneel and worship the Lord. Saints, I have good news for you. Praising God can be done at home, in your car or anywhere else you may be. To commune intimately, the altar in front of the church is a definite place to be.

Psalm 95: 6: "O come, let us worship and bow down, let us kneel before the Lord our maker."

The prophets of the Old Testament built altars to God. At these altars, the prophets cried out and repented to God for the sins of the people as well as for their own sins. At the altars, the prophets repented and offered blood sacrifices on behalf of the people and their sacrifices were accepted by God.

We no longer need to offer sacrifices because God made the ultimate sacrifice for our sins through his shed blood.

Matthew 26: 28: "For this is my blood of the New Testament, which is shed for many for the remission of sins."

When we are convicted of sin we need to repent and the best place to repent is at the altar. If it is possible, we should kneel at a dedicated church altar.

It means a lot to have an altar. We need to have an altar in our homes so we can talk to God and have a place to be with him.

Do not be ashamed to come to this altar. God will meet you there. Don't be mistaken, he will meet you while you are in a seat. BUT, there is something about a sanctified and often used altar. At the altar you can humble yourself, raise your hands and cry out unto God. Say to the Lord, 'Here I am. Take me and use me for your glory.'

WORSHIP HIM SINCERLY

WITH ALL YOUR HEART, you need to mean what you pray. God is looking for people who will love and praise him. God is looking for people who will come back to him and turn from their wicked ways. We need to worship God in Spirit and in truth.

2 Chronicles 7: 14: "If my people, which are called by my name shall humble themselves and pray and seek my face and turn from their wicked ways; then I will hear from heaven and will forgive their sin and will heal their land."

John 4: 23-24: "But the hour cometh and now is, when true worshippers shall worship the Father in Spirit and in truth; for the Father seeketh such to worship him. God is a Spirit and they that worship him must worship him in truth and spirit."

Be truthful and honest with God. Don't kneel at the altar and say 'Ruth did wrong or Clay did wrong.' Instead say to God; "Lord I am in need of prayer. I have sinned and am standing in the need of forgiveness.' Only after you have asked for forgiveness can you forgive others. Forgive those who you have something against.

The Lord is looking for a people of deliverance. Blind eyes will be opened and ears will hear what the Spirit of the Lord is saying to the churches.

Revelation 2: 7: "He that hath an ear let him hear what the Spirit saith unto the churches. To him that overcometh will I give to eat of the tree of life, which is in the midst of the paradise of God."

If you could only see the glories of heaven and what awaits you there, you would be sure you are saved by the blood of Jesus. Here on earth we go through many trials and tribulations in our everyday life. Quite often it seems the enemy tries to steal everything from us, but thankfully God gives us the patience to endure and ultimately win the victory.

1 Corinthians 15: 57: "But thanks be to God, which giveth us the victory through our Lord Jesus Christ."

As we all know there are many pressures in life but there is peace and safety in our Lord.

I beseech any of you that don't have a spirit filled church to find one that preaches the Word of God and in power of the almighty to transform our hearts and lives. Be sure the church you find believes in the power of the Holy Spirit. When you find such a church you will be taught the wisdom of God and you can be set free from grief, troubles and sorrows.

It is imperative that we meet together with Gods people.

Hebrews 12: 5: "You should not stay away from the church meetings, as some are doing, but you should meet together and encourage each other. Do this even more as you see the day coming."

Don't try to be out in the world all alone without God and others. There are saints of God who love you but remember God loves you.

GLORIES TO BE REVEALED

THERE ARE MYSTERIES TO be revealed in another part of the glories of heaven. These I was not allowed to see.

Matthew 13: 11: "...because it is given unto you to know the mysteries of the kingdom of heaven, but to them it is not given."

In heaven I saw beautiful mansions and houses. Being in this section I felt the tour went by very fast. From this section I was taken to another. Here the angels were doing all kinds of tasks. In an orderly manner they came from earth and entered the gates with papers in their hands.

Instead of papers some of the angels were carrying books in their hands in which they wrote different things. Set aside were certain areas, in heaven, in which the angels took the reports to. Whether the angels carried books or papers, the reports were logged into a book to keep records of the saint's rewards. As a child of God, you will be rewarded for whatever you do for Jesus Christ sake, once you obtain your place in heaven. I am writing this book for the sake of the Lord Jesus Christ and for his honor and glory.

Habakkuk 2: 2: "...write down the vision and make it plain..."

My hope is for you to understand the mysteries of heaven. I am unable to share all the mysteries with you because some were kept from me.

1 Corinthians 13: 9: "For we know in part and prophesy in part."

O happy day when we reach our final destination, our final home because there all questions will be answered, all our prayers answered and all our deepest desires will be fulfilled.

Job 13: 3: "...I desire to reason with God."

2 Corinthians 5: 2: "...earnestly desiring to be clothed upon with our house which is in heaven."

VISIONS OF ANGELS AT WORK

*T*HIS SECTION IS ABOUT angels at work. There are so many beautiful things that I saw that I want to share with you. I am praying to give you some delight and joy in knowing what awaits you as you work for the Lord.

Amos 3: 7: "...he revealeth his secrets unto his servants, the prophets."

To those who will be sensitive to Gods revelations and who will proclaim his message, God will show these things.

Isaiah 44: 6-8: "The Lord, the King of Israel is the Lord All Powerful, who saves Israel. This is what he says;" I am the beginning and the end. I am the only God. Who is a god like me? That god should come and prove it. Let him tell and explain all that has happened since I set up my ancient people. He should also tell what will happen in the future. Don't be afraid! Don't worry! I have always told you what will happen. You are my witnesses. There is no other god but me. I know of no other Rock, I am the only One."

The Lord answered and said to me write down this vision and write it clearly so whoever reads it can run to tell others.

In the Word of God there are many scriptural examples about God wanting to reveal things to us through his chosen representatives. The Word of God is sure and true.

Psalm 119: 160: "Thy word is true…"

There are several prophets in the Bible that had visions from the Lord.

DANIEL: We read in Daniel 7: 1: "…Daniel had a dream. He saw visions as he was lying on his bed…"

JOHN, the Revelator, also saw visions of the Lord.

Revelation 1: 11: "…write what you see in a book…"

ISAIAH was a great prophet with a very important message for Judah because of his visions and his courage in telling them.

Isaiah 1: 1: "The vision of Isaiah the son of Amos, which he saw concerning Judah…"

EZEKIEL was called and anointed for a prophetic ministry because he saw visions of God."

REVEALING GODS TRUTH

MY FIRST EXPERIENCE WAS when God choose to show me hell. God was wearing a sparkling white robe which was full of light and power, the first time I met him. He was much taller than myself, had a very well trimmed beard and on his shoulders rested his thick hair. God's eyes were very piercing, like they could penetrate through a person.

Jesus Christ will go to great length to show a person heaven and hell and things to come because of his great love and compassion.

CHARIOTS OF FIRE

*L*ET'S LOOK AND SEE what the Bible says about the chariot of fire. 2 Kings 6: 17: "Then Elisha prayed, 'Lord Open my servants eyes and let him see. The Lord opened the eyes of the young man and he saw that the mountain was full of horses and chariots of fire all around Elisha."

During my trip to heaven I saw chariots of fire with angels driving these chariots. These chariots were very large vehicles and I was greatly surprised by their splendor.

REVELATIONS OF GOD

ERE IS A VERSE about angels Acts 1: 10: "And while they looked steadfastly towards heaven as he went up, behold, two men stood by them in white apparel." How can anyone read this verse and not believe it? God openly showed angels to his people when Jesus was caught up into heaven.

Saints!! Do you realize that God wants to reveal his glorious works to us in these last days? He wants to show us visions and he wants to communicate these truths to us so we may become stimulated and have great pleasure about working for God on earth.

MIRACLES IN CHURCHES

I SAW ANGELS EVERYWHERE AS I was worshipping during a church service and in their hands they held golden swords.

The Lord spoke to me in an audible voice and said; "Child I want to heal certain physical as people come during the church service. I want this to be a sign to the fact that heaven is real."

Acts 4: 30: "…that signs and wonders may be done by the name of thy holy child, Jesus."

I saw angels writing things down in a large book and excitement filled my heart. It seemed to me as if the ceiling opened up and I could see the throne of God. Angels were singing and praising God as they surrounded the throne.

BREAKING THE BONDAGE OF SIN

I SAW ANGELS MINGLING IN the congregation nudging people to give their hearts to the Lord, as the pastor gave the altar call. As the angels touched the individuals and as they gave their hearts to God I saw the blackest, dirtiest sins began to stir violently and out of their hearts as they cried and prayed to God. This was a beautiful sight to behold.

In my spirit I could see the chains that had enwrapped these people but as they received forgiveness the angels would break the bonds, shatter the chains and cast them off. The final bands were broken by Gods own hands as the people raised their hands and confessed their sins.

There was a lot of shouting, crying and praising God as they stood to their feet because now their hearts, souls and minds were now free. It was wonderful to see.

In services all over the world God provided great miracles and wonderful deliverance took place.

I stood at the altar, myself, praising God for his miracles, signs and wonders. The angels were helping in the ministry of the Lord Jesus Christ.

BREAKING THE BONDAGE

S THE PREACHER SPOKE the word of God the words took on the form of a sword. This sword would pierce a person's body and go straight to the problem to heal it.

The glory of God overwhelmed me because it was everywhere and I praised God for the blessings of heaven on earth and the beautiful revelation of his word.

THE WORD OF GOD

THE ANGELS WERE DOING many beautiful things in the church services where people were praising the Lord. If you have read the Word of god you know that angels are ministering spirits of the Lord sent forth to minister to the heirs of salvation.

Hebrews 1: 14: "Are they not all ministering spirits sent forth to minister for them who shall be heirs of salvation?"

Revelation 1: 10: "I was in the Spirit on the Lord's day…"

At a service I attended I saw a minister prophesying and God opened my eyes to see an angel over his head. Out of a horn the angel poured a mixture of fire and oil over the preachers head. Through a vision I saw the preacher's heart and it was full of the Word of God. As he preached the word came up from his heart, then into his throat and then out of his mouth. I could see every word that came out of his mouth was like a two-edged sword. There was an angel recording every word the minister spoke.

'This is your word going forth, O God.'

An angel was holding the Holy Scriptures and as the minister preached the Word of God the word seemed to leap off the pages of the Bible. From his heart and out of his mouth the words flowed. This minister was so filled with the Spirit of god that the words he spoke became the two-edged sword.

Revelation 1: 16: "…out of his mouth went a two-edged sword…"

Hebrews 4: 12: "For the word of God is quick and powerful and sharper than any two-edged sword…"

As people stood at the altar and the minister prayed and laid hands upon the sick or the ones who were afflicted with diseases, the Lord allowed me to see whatever the affliction was, no matter what part of the body it was. I was a witness to many miraculous healings through the healing power of God. I saw the sword of the word as it went to the afflicted area of the person. As the sword went through the afflicted area heat would pulsate through the person's body. I was allowed to watch as the affliction left their bodies. After the healing prayer bestowed upon them, many said they had felt the heat as it pulsated through their bodies.

James 5: 15: "And the prayer that is said with faith will make the sick person well; the Lord will heal that person."

The Lord allowed me to see, spiritually, how the diseases were burnt out of the person's body. It was miraculous and beautiful how the revelation of God's word began to work. I began to praise the Lord as I saw new cells and new skin began to grow where the old, diseased, rotten parts had been.

Shouting and praising God could be heard for miles around because people had been healed. On earth we only know and see in part. We are only allowed to hear and see what God wants us to. God permitted me to see what he wanted me to see and I give him the credit, honor and glory.

APPROACHING THE THRONE

OT ONLY WERE PROPHETS in Biblical times important, they are necessary in today's world. There is a fivefold ministry spoken of in Ephesians that I began to see the importance of.

Ephesians 4: 11-12: "And Christ gave gifts to people—he made some to be apostles, some to be prophets, some to go and tell the Good News and some to have the work of caring for and teaching Gods people. Christ gave those gifts to prepare Gods holy people for the work of serving, to make the body of Christ stronger.

This same verse in the King James Bible states it like this: "And he gave some apostles, and some prophets and some evangelists and some pastors and teachers; For the perfecting of the saints, for the work of the ministry, for the edifying of the body of Christ."

I became aware of how important each person is in the body of Christ.

Hebrews 4: 16 tells us we can "…come boldly unto the throne of grace that we may obtain mercy and find grace to help in the time of need."

The book of Hebrews goes on to tell us in Hebrews 10: 19 that "...we are completely free to enter the Most Holy Place without fear because of the blood of Jesus' death."

Hebrews 9: 22: "And almost all things are by law purged with blood; and without shedding of blood is no remission."

Friends, family and saints, I can attest this is true. The blood of Jesus Christ made an atonement for our souls. In grace his word and his blood work together.

Hebrews 4:16: "...come boldly unto the throne of grace; that we may obtain mercy and find grace to help in time of need."

A VERY PRESENT HELP

OW MANY TIMES DO we have great needs? How often do we have sickness in our bodies? How often do we have heartaches? Are we going through a divorce or has a loved one died? Has one of our children strayed? Does it seem like we have no money coming in and we need help? But, do you know we can come boldly before the throne of God and pray 'I need your help, Lord.'

The Lord is always there when we cry out to him. I saw an angel with a giant Bible in his hands. After the angel opened the Bible he shoved it in Satan's face. Satan would not be there in his own form but he would be there as an evil spirit or serpent. As the angel opened up the Word of God the devil literally fell backwards because he knew the angel was using the two-edged sword against him.

I want to thank God that Jesus Christ defeated Satan once and for all, at the cross, so we may have life and freedom.

Colossians 2: 15: "...with the cross, he won the victory..."

Because of Jesus death on the cross we can now come boldly to the throne of grace wherever we are.

Hebrews 5: 16: "Let us, then, feel very sure that we can come before Gods throne where there is grace. There we can receive mercy and grace to help us when we need it."

ANOINTING AND HEALING

*T*HROUGH THE HOLY SCRIPTURES we know God's mercy and grace is real and that he is present to heal our every sickness and disease. I encourage you to delve into the Word of God and learn what his promises are.

Go boldly to the throne of God and ask him to help you when you have a need.

Hebrews 1: 14: "All the angels are spirits who serve God and are sent to help those who will receive salvation."

I believe this scripture and I know it for a fact. I saw this many times, on my trip to heaven, that when we call out to the Lord, God's sends angels to help us in the power and might of His Word and His Spirit.

Under the mighty power of God, demons were cast out. As these demons were cast out, they came out in the appearance of dark shadows and apparitions.

Acts 4: 12: "...there is none other name under heaven among men..."

When Jesus' name was called on, I watched as the angel took the evil spirit and bound it with a chain.

Oh Lord Jesus, how beautiful your word is to deliver these demons from the possessed people with evil problems and from the evil powers of the devil.

It is only by the Word of God that demons can be cast out. Jesus Christ word and his word alone. Only through the mighty name of Jesus will this work.

Jesus Christ will save you, if you will call upon his name. You will be born again, set free from your sins and you will have an eternal home in heaven.

2 Corinthians 5: 2: "For in this groan, earnestly desiring to be clothed upon with our house which is in heaven."

THE POWER OF THE WORD

*T*HROUGH A VISION I saw millions of people hungry for the Lord and I could tell there was going to be a mighty move of God. Coming down like rain was the glory of God.

I could see the Holy Spirit moving in the midst of the people and saving them.

Ephesians 2: 8: "For by grace are ye saved through faith…"

Many fell under the power of Jesus Christ as they accepted the Lord. If they were standing they fell backwards or if they were seated they fell from their seats. As the Lord's power surged through their bodies a new transformation took place and they were delivered. As the presence of the Lord came down there was much joy. The preaching of God's word set these people free.

I had never seen this many people hungry for the word of God. They wanted to be born again, have Jesus in their hearts and be free from the bondage of sin. The power of God is incredible.

FOOD FOR THOUGHT

*T*HINK ON THIS SCRIPTURE:
Exodus 14: 19-20: "And the angel of God which went before the camp of Israel, removed and went behind them, and the pillar of the cloud went from before their faces and stood behind them. And it came between the camp of the Egyptians and the camp of Israel; and it was a cloud and darkness to them, but it gave light by night to these; so that the one came not near the other all night."

Don't you know saints of God that he wants to perform miracles today just as he did in the past?

Luke 7: 21: "And in the same hour he cured many of their inflictions and plagues and of evil spirits; and unto many that were blind he gave sight."

Hebrews 13: 8: "Jesus Christ the same yesterday, today and forever."

Being that this verse is true, we as the children of God can expect God to perform mighty miracles for us in this day and time. Go to him in prayer and he will answer. We as humans have been eliminating the benefits God has provided for us. All the beautiful things God has given us, we have neglected.

Here are some verses that verify Gods willingness to answer us when we cry out to him.

Philippians 4: 19: "But my God shall supply all your need according to his riches in glory by Christ Jesus."

Jeremiah 32: 17: "Behold I am the Lord…is there anything too hard for me?"

John 14: 14: "If ye shall ask anything in my name, I will do it."

James 1: 17: "Every good gift and every perfect gift is from above."

1 Peter 5: 7: "Casting all your care upon Him; for he careth for you."

In today's world there are mediums, fortune tellers, psychics and all kind of witchcraft. You can't turn your television or computer on without an advertisement of someone promising all things of things, from fame to lucky numbers. They are feeding on the hunger in people's hearts. People are seeking advice and direction for their lives through all kinds of sources. But, saints, I am here to tell you that God is real and true and that he does not want us to follow after these other physics, fortune-tellers etc. it is God's desire for us that we do not see the evils of witchcraft and the occult that is prevalent in the world today.

In the book of Leviticus God speaks against the occult and seeking after familiar spirits.

Leviticus 19: 31: "Do not go to mediums or fortune tellers for advice or you will become unclean. I am the Lord your God."

Deuteronomy 18: 10: "...Don't let anyone use magic or witchcraft or try to explain the meaning of signs."

Saints; know how very wrong it is to go to physics and mediums for guidance and help. God's angels are real and are sent to minister to us who are heirs of salvation.

Psalm 91: 11: "For he shall give his angels charge over thee, to keep thee in all thy ways."

Isaiah 63: 9: "In all their afflictions he was afflicted and the angel of his presence saved them; in his love and in his pity he redeemed them and he bare them and carried them all the days of old."

Daniel 3: 28: "Then Nebuchadnezzar said, "Praise the god of Shadrach, Meshach and Abednego. Their God has sent his angel and saved his servants from the fire. These three men trusted their God and refused to obey my command. They were willing to die rather than serve or worship any other god other than their own."

TROOPS OF ANGELS

THROUGH MY SPIRITUAL EYES I could see the Word of God written in the sky, as it surrounded my home.

There was a great assemblage of angels everywhere you looked around my house. Some were sitting, talking amongst themselves while another group with commanding eyes stood watching. Yet another group of angels stood wing tip to wing tip with their backs towards the house. This last group was made up of the biggest angels and they reminded me of warriors. All these huge angels had a sword at his side. Not even a dark shadow could creep towards my house because the angels would pull their swords and defend me and my family.

Saints, in Ephesians 6: 17: it says: "The sword of the spirit…is the word of God."

Please Remember this!!!

Hebrews 4: 12: "God's word is alive and working and is sharper than a double-edged sword…"

Malachi 4: 3: "And ye shall tread down the wicked; for they shall be ashes under the soles of your feet…"

It surprised me greatly that I was able to see the Word of God in action.

The angels delivered Peter when God sent his word.

Acts 12: 7-11: "Suddenly an angel of the Lord stood there and a light shined on the cell. The angel struck Peter on the side and woke him up; Hurry! Get Up! The angel said. And the chains fell off Peter's hands. Then the angel told him; "Get dresses and put on your sandals. And Peter did. Then the angel said; Put on your coat and follow me. So Peter followed him out but he did not know if what the angel was doing was real; he thought he might be seeing a vision. They went past the first and second guards and came to the iron gate that separated them from the city. The gate opened by itself for them, and they went through it. When they had walked down one street the angel suddenly left him. Then Peter realized what had happened. He thought, 'Now I know that the Lord really sent his angel to me. He rescued me from Herod and from all the things the Jewish people thought would happen.

ANGELS AND THE WORD

ERE ARE BUT A few of the Scriptures where angels appeared to men.

Genesis 32: 1: "When Jacob also went his way, the angel of God met him."

Numbers 22: 31: "Then the Lord let Balaam see the angel of the Lord…then Balaam bowed face down on the ground."

1 King 19: 5"…suddenly an angel came to him and touched him…"

Matthew 1: 20: "While Joseph thought about these things, an angel of the Lord came to him in a dream. The angel said; 'Joseph, descendant of David, don't be afraid to take Mary as your wife, because the baby in her is from the Holy Spirit."

John 20: 12: "She saw two angels dressed in white sitting where Jesus body had been, one at the head and one at the foot."

Acts 8: 26: "An angel of the Lord said to Phillip; 'Get ready and go south to the road that leads down to Gaza from Jerusalem, the desert road."

Acts 27: 23: "Last night an angel came to me from God I belong to and worship."

As children of God we need to understand how much protection we have. Another thing we must understand is that God has provided everything for us through his Holy Word. Saints, we can go to him boldly when we need help and in our times of need.

In the name of Jesus Christ we may ask him for help, at the throne of grace. When you or I go ask for assistance, God will always give it. He loves us so much that it is a joy to him to help us if we keep his commandments and serve him.

A NEW WORLD IS COMING

I WAS DESPERATELY SICK FOR a few days after my trip to hell. I was afraid to turn the lights off at nights and at all times I had my Bible near me, reading it constantly. My soul was in severe shock because I had experienced some of what the lost endured when they go to hell.

Jesus would calm me with these words in Mark 4: 39: "…Peace be still…"

As soon as he said these words peace flooded my soul but nonetheless within a few moments I would again be hysterical and screaming in fear.

Even though I would go through periods of hysteria I knew that Jesus was there with me. But even with that knowledge I sometimes could not feel his presence. Fear would overtake me and I feared going back to hell.

When I returned from my trip to hell I tried to tell others of my experiences but they would not listen. Because of what I had seen I begged anyone who would listen. I would tell them they needed to repent of their sins before it was too late. The torment and tortures I went through while in hell were difficult for others to understand or believe. Also I had tried to tell them of other things God had shown me, but to no avail. They shut their ears.

The Lord reassured me with some scriptures that he heals:

1 Peter 2: 24: "…by whose stripes we are healed."

Luke 5: 17: "…and the power of the Lord was present to heal them."

Isaiah 53: 5: "…and with his stripes we are healed."

2 Kings 20: 5: "…I will heal thee…"

Exodus 15: 26: "…I am the Lord that healeth thee."

At first I was not fully convinced I would recover completely, but thank God, complete healing did come.

PARADISE OF PEACE

HILE I WAS WITH Jesus, he said to me; "Come I want to show you the love and goodness of God and parts of heaven. The wondrous works of the Lord, I want you to see because they are so beautiful to behold."

'See the goodness and kindness of the Lord your God for his mercy endures forever;' an angel said to me.

Psalm 104: 31: "The glory of the Lord shall endure for ever…"

There was such a sense of love and tenderness about the angel that tears filled my eyes and I wept because never in my life had I felt such love and tenderness. The angel spoke to me and said: "Behold the majesty, power and might of the Lord. Let me show you the place he has created for the children."

John 14: 2: "In my Father's house are many mansions; if it were not so, I would have told you. I go to prepare a place for you."

Before my eyes a large planet loomed and it appeared to be as large as the earth.

Revelation 21: 1-2: "Then I saw a new heaven and a new earth. The first had disappeared and there was no sea anymore. And I saw the holy city, the New Jerusalem, coming down out of heaven from God. It was prepared like a bride dressed for her husband."

Shortly after the angel spoke to me, the Father, himself, spoke to me. He said: "The Father, the Son, and the Holy Spirit are one. The Father and the Holy Spirit are one and the Father and the Son are one. I sent my only begotten Son to die on the cross so no one needs to be lost."

Colossians 2: 13: "When you were spiritually dead because of your sins and because you were not free from the power of your sinful self, God made you alive with Christ, and he forgave all sins."

"My dear child, I am about to show you the place I made for the children because of my great love for them. My heart grieves for a mother who has lost her child. I seen the miscarriage you had. You see, I know all things and care.

From the moment of conception, I know. I know of the mothers who have aborted their child, I know of other mothers who have snuffed the life from their living child. So many unwanted children. I know the children born with crippling defects and the ones who are stillborn. From the moment of conception each and every one of them is a soul.

I send my angels down to earth to bring me the children when they die. Once in heaven they are loved and they become perfect beings. The child is made whole and whatever body part is missing, I restore. They are given perfect bodies."

A sense of well-being and a feeling of being loved penetrated this entire large planet. No matter where you looked everything was perfect. Mingled among the lush green grass and pools of crystal clear water were marble seats and highly polished benches to sit upon. Looking around I could see children engaging in all types of activities and each wore a white robe and sandals. These white robes were the purest I had ever seen and in the light of this planet the robes sparkled. Everywhere, a great abundance of color emphasized the whiteness of each child's robe. Angels were keepers of the entrance and written in a book was each child's name.

From a golden book children were being taught music and the Word of God. At this angelic school, it really amazed me to see animals of all kinds stroll up to the children, romp with them and then sit down beside them.

Abounding everywhere was joy and happiness and not a tear nor sorrow could be seen. Everything was supremely beautiful and no words on earth could describe the beauty.

"Look before you;" the angel said.

There before me was another planet that glowed like a massive light. With the radiance of a million stars; this light shone and everything on this planet was beautiful and alive.

Two mountains of pure gold were in the distance, while nearer to me were two golden gates. In these gates diamonds and other precious stones were embedded. Lying before me, in its entire splendor, was the city New Jerusalem—the city of God as it will come down to earth. I knew, beyond a shadow of a doubt, that this was the new earth. Read Revelation 21: 1-2 again.

EARTH AGAIN

BEFORE I KNEW IT I was back viewing the old earth but the earth after the Great Tribulation but before the final fires of Armageddon that will ultimately purge it. As I looked I saw Jerusalem, the capital city of the millennium.

In my vision, I saw people coming from far and near making their way toward the Holy city. Here, in the Holy city was Jesus the King. From every nation of the earth people brought him gifts and paid him respect, recognizing God King of Kings.

The Lord knew I was confused so he gave me an interpretation and a greater clarity to my vision.

"Soon I will return and the righteous shall be taken to heaven first.

1 Thessalonians 4: 16-17: "For the Lord himself shall descend from heaven with a shout, with the voice of the archangel and with the trump of God; and the dead in Christ shall rise first. Then the ones who are alive will be caught up with Me to heaven. Then we which are alive and remain shall be caught up together with them in the clouds to meet the Lord in the air…"

After the righteous have been raised then the Antichrist will reign upon the earth for an appointed time and there will be tribulations such as have been before and will never be again.

The Lord continued speaking and said; "I will return with my saints and Satan will be cast into a bottomless pit, where he will remain for a thousand years.

Revelation 20: 2-3: "The angel grabbed the dragon, the old snake, who is the devil and Satan and tied him up for a thousand years. Then he threw him into the bottomless pit, closed it and locked it over him. The angel did this so he could not trick the people of the earth anymore until the thousand years were ended. After a thousand years he must be set free for a short time."

The Lord said to me;" I will reign over the earth Jerusalem during the thousand years. When the millenniums is past Satan will be released for a season and I will defeat him will the brightness of my coming. The old earth will pass away and behold there shall be a new earth and a New Jerusalem coming down upon it and I will reign forever and ever."

Revelation 21: 1-2: "Then I saw a new heaven and a new earth. The first heaven and the first earth had disappeared and there is no sea anymore. And I saw the holy city, the New Jerusalem, coming down out of heaven from God…"

THE RETURN OF CHRIST

I saw the coming of the Lord in my vision. His call sounded like trumpets and the voice of an archangel.

1 Thessalonians 4: 16: "For the Lord himself shall descend from heaven with a shout, with the voice of an archangel, and the trump of God…"

The whole earth shook and out of the graves came the righteous to meet their Lord in the air.

The blare of the trumpets went on continually for a very long time. The earth and the sea gave up their dead.

Revelation 20: 13: "And the sea gave up the dead which were in it and death and hell delivered up the dead which were in them…"

I saw the Lord standing on the top of the clouds in garments of fire and beholding the glorious scene. Again I heard the trumpets blaring. An incredible thing happened as I watched. Those who were alive, in Christ, and remained on earth ascended to meet him.

1 Thessalonians 4: 14-17: "For if we believe that Jesus died and rose again, even so them also which

sleep in Jesus will God bring with him. For this we say unto you by the word of the Lord, that we which are alive and remain unto the coming of the Lord shall not prevent them which are asleep. For the Lord himself shall descend from heaven with a shout, with the voice of the archangel and with the trump of God: and the dead in Christ shall rise first: then we which remain shall be caught up together with them in the clouds, to meet the Lord in the air: and so shall we ever be with the Lord."

Millions upon millions of the redeemed converged on a gathering place. As each redeemed person reached that point an angel clothed them in robes of purest white. All through the crowd great rejoicing could be heard. The angels were everywhere and giving special attention to the risen ones because it is the angels' responsibility to serve. The redeemed were given new glorified bodies and were transformed as they passed through the air.

THE BODY OF CHRIST

During my vision I seen, in the heavens, a spiritual body of great size. I knew in my spirit it was the body of Christ. Dripping to the earth was the blood of Christ as he lay on his back. This represented our Lord's slain body. God's body grew and grew until it surrounded, completely, the heavens. Millions of redeemed were going into it.

I stood in wonder as millions climbed up a staircase to the body and filled it, beginning with the feet and continuing through the legs, arms, stomach, heart and the head.

When it was full, I saw it was filled from every corner of the earth. In unison the millions of people lifted their voice in praise.

Revelation 5: 9-10: "And they sang a new song to the Lamb: You are worthy to take the scroll and to open its seals, because you were killed and with the blood of your death you bought people for God from every tribe, language, people and nation. You made them to be a kingdom of priests for our God and they will rule on the earth."

Around the throne millions of people were gathered. Angels brought the books from which judgment was read and before the mercy seat rewards were given to many.

Standing before the throne I was astonished at what happened. Darkness covered the face of the earth and demon forces went everywhere. From their prison countless evil spirits were loosed and they spilled forth onto the earth. I heard a voice saying: "... woe to the inhibiters of the earth and of the sea! For the devil is come down unto you having great wrath, because he knoweth that he hath but a short time." Revelation 12: 12.

THE WRATH OF GOD

I SAW AN ANGRY BEAST and he spewed his venom upon all the earth. Hell shook in his fury and from the bottomless pit a swarming horde of evil creatures appeared and blackened the earth with their immense numbers.

Revelation 6: 12: "...there was a great earthquake; and the sun became black as sackcloth of hair, and the moon became as blood."

Men and women fled into the hills, caves and mountains. Upon the earth were wars, famine and death. From the east, west, north and south horses and chariots of fire appeared in the heavens.

"Hear, O Earth, the King is Coming;" an angel announced.

The King of Kings and Lord of Lords appeared in the sky. Saints of all ages, clad in the purest white were with him in glorious splendor.

Revelation 1: 7: "...every eye shall see him."

Romans 14: 11: "...every knee shall bow and every tongue shall confess to God."

The angels put in their sickles and harvested the ripened grain which is the end of the world.

Revelation 14: 14-19: "Then I looked and there before me was a white cloud and sitting on the white cloud was one who looked like a Son of Man. He had a gold crown on his head and a sharp sickle in his hand. Then another angel came out of the temple and called out in a loud voice to the sitting on the cloud; 'Take your sickle and harvest from the earth because the time to harvest has come and the fruit of the earth is ripe. So the one sitting on the cloud swung his sickle over the earth and the earth was harvested. Then another angel came out of the temple in heaven and he also had a sharp sickle. And then another angel who has power over the fire came from the altar. This angel called to the angel with the sharp sickle saying; 'Take your sharp sickle and gather the bunches of grapes from the earths' vine, because its grapes are ripe. Then the angel swung his sickle over the earth. He gathered the earths' grapes and threw them into the great winepress of God's anger.'

The King is coming, so we must love one another, be firm in the truth and correct our children in the light of the soon coming of Christ.

THE LORDS FINAL PLEA: BE READY

"REPENT AND BE READY for the kingdom of God is at hand;" Jesus said to me.

Matthew 3: 2: "…Repent ye, for the kingdom of heaven is at hand."

Prepare the way of the Lord for my will and my word will be performed; Jesus said to me.

1 Timothy 6: 17: "Command those who are rich with things of this world not to be proud. Tell them to hope in God not in their uncertain riches."

Galatians 5: 16: "…Live by following the Spirit. Then you will not do what your sinful selves want."

Galatians 6: 7-9: "Do not be fooled; you cannot cheat God. People only harvest what they plant. If they plant to satisfy their sinful selves, their sinful selves will bring them ruin, but, if they plant to please the Spirit, they will receive eternal life from the Spirit."

Galatians 5: 19-24: "Now the works of the flesh are manifest, which are these, adultery, fornication, uncleanness, lasciviousness, idolatry, witchcraft, hatred, variance, emulations, wrath, strife, seditions, heresies. Envying, murders, drunkenness, revellings and such like: of the which I tell you before, as I have also told you in time past, that they which do such things shall not inherit the kingdom of God.

But the fruit of the Spirit is love, joy, peace, longsuffering, gentleness, goodness, faith, meekness, temperance: against such there is no law. And they that are Christ' have crucified the flesh with the affections and lusts. If we live in the Spirit, let us also walk in the Spirit."

Continuing to speak to me Jesus said; "The end will come when the Word of God is fulfilled. No man knows the day or hour when the Son of God will return to earth. Not even the son knows only by the Father.

Matthew 25: 13: "…ye know neither the day nor the hour wherein the Son of Man cometh."

Saints, the word is quickly being fulfilled. Come as a little child and let God cleanse you from the works of the flesh.

Here is a little prayer you could say:

"Lord Jesus, come into my heart and forgive me of my sins. I know I am a sinner and I repent of my sins. Wash me in your blood and make me clean. I have sinned against heaven and before you and am worthy to be called your daughter/son. I receive you by faith as my Savior."

God spoke once again and said: "I will give you pastors after my own heart, and I will be your shepherd. I will be your God and you will be my people. Read the word of God and do not forsake the assembling of yourselves together. Give your whole life to me and I will keep you. I will never leave you or forsake you."

Hebrews 13: 5: "...I will never leave you, nor forsake you."

BE READY TO MEET GOD

*I*N THIS BOOK I have shared with you, from the depths of my heart, the many visions and revelations of heaven that were given to me by the power of God. ***GOD LOVES YOU!!*** Remember that!!! He has shown his care and great love by sending forth his mighty word to us and granting us revelations in these last days.

Children of God, we must be ready to meet the Lord. At all times we must be looking for his coming. We are in a season of troubles, as we all know. Never in the life of history has there been an era like this.

Again, implore you from the depths of my heart to be ready for his coming because we do not know the day or hour when the God will return. ***JESUS CHRIST IS COMING BACK!!!***

If we live righteously in Christ Jesus we will meet our loved ones at the gates of glory as we go in.

Are you receiving this beautiful message in your heart?

Earlier on I told you about the books and records that the angels keep. Everything we do for Jesus' sake is recorded and once we get to heaven our rewards are going to be much greater than they are on earth. Each and every deed we do is written down by the angels.

To carry the cross of Jesus Christ many times teachers, preachers, evangelists and other leaders have to temporarily leave spouses, children and homes. The Lord sees this and knows all about it and he also knows about the numerous times we go somewhere and are not treated as the children of the Lord. No matter how much we are mistreated we are still the Kings' children.

We are still to be servants. God wants us to serve one another as he served us.

God didn't promise us a rose garden, he never promised us splendor on earth, but we can have riches, blessings, honor and material as God permits. If we take up our cross and follow Jesus we can have these things.

Listen, I want you to be ready. If you have never received Jesus Christ as your Savior, you can be saved according to the Holy Scriptures.

John 3: 16: "For God so loved the world that he gave his only begotten Son, that whosoever believeth in him should not perish but have everlasting life."

Romans 10: 9-10 and 13: "That if thou shalt confess with thy mouth the Lord Jesus and shalt believe in thine heart, that God raised him from the dead, thou shalt be saved. For with the heart man believeth unto righteousness; and with the mouth confession is made unto salvation. For whosoever shall call upon the name of the Lord shall be saved."

If it your desire to get right with God, please pray this prayer:

"Father, in the name of Jesus Christ I come unto you, just as I am; a sinner. I have sinned against you and against heaven. I ask you, Lord Jesus, to forgive me and to come into my heart and save my soul. Cleanse me from all unrighteousness. Lord Jesus, let me be born again by the spirit of the Loving God. I give my life to you, Lord Jesus. I believe that you are the Son of God and I believe that you are Jesus Christ who was sent to save my soul from hell. I give you thanks, praise and honor. Amen"

if you have prayed this prayer with me and really believed what you prayed, you are now saved. You have asked Jesus Christ into your heart, now begin to confess him with your lips and praise him.

To God, be praise and honor.

PLEASE, PLEASE, PLEASE, from the depths of my heart I implore you to accept Jesus Christ before it's too late. We are not guaranteed a tomorrow.

ACCEPT THE LORD TODAY!!!!!